"From the horrors of his story as a survivor of the genocide in Rwanda, Ntamushobora provides an African perspective on issues of injustice, racism, ethnic conflict, and violations of human rights. . . . He leads the reader to think in fresh ways about what it means to love God and love our neighbors as ourselves."

—SHERWOOD LINGENFELTER
Professor and Provost Emeritus, Fuller Theological Seminary

"In this book Faustin shares much of his story and how God has used people, very different from him, to transform his life. God wants to do this for us too. As you read this book I am sure God will use it to open your eyes so you can see and experience the transformational impact others are having on you—for the glory of God."

—W. MATTHEW REED JR.
Pastor of Missional and Adult Ministries, Calvary Church

"Faustin Ntamushobora, pastor, scholar, and compelling story-teller, eloquently describes *ubuntu* theology, centered in restorative justice based upon forgiveness. Sharing heart-wrenching personal stories as a Rwandan genocide survivor, as well as spiritual, intellectual, and cultural eurekas in the discovery of the different other, the author unfolds the only salve for the problem of the human heart: the transformative work of Jesus Christ, healer and hope of the nations."

—JUNE HETZEL
Dean of Education, Biola University

"Today, discourses between Africa and the rest of the world, particularly the West, haven't quite sobered up. Such encounters, fueled by the problem of active exclusion and rubbishing of each other's perspectives, often raise their voices in blame-games and grandstanding. . . . Ntamushobora introduces *ubuntu* not only as the distinguishing principle that separates Africa from the rest of the world, but he also presents it as the hermeneutic key to the question of race, self-understanding of Africa, and a basis for contemplation of transformation as something that happens through 'the different other.'"

—James Kombo
Deputy Vice Chancellor, Academic Affairs, Daystar University

Transformation Through the Different Other

Transformation Through the Different Other

the Different Other

A Rendezvous of Giving and Receiving

FAUSTIN NTAMUSHOBORA

WIPF & STOCK · Eugene, Oregon

TRANSFORMATION THROUGH THE DIFFERENT OTHER
A Rendezvous of Giving and Receiving

Wipf & Stock
An Imprint of Wipf and Stock Publishers
199 W. 8th Ave., Suite 3
Eugene, OR 97401
www.wipfandstock.com

ISBN 13: 978-1-62032-776-0
Manufactured in the U.S.A.

My mum, Ntawurutwayenda (Rose),

*for your dedication to Christ from the time you
surrendered your life to Him until now at 90 years old,
for teaching me that forgiveness is a liberating power that
is found at the cross of Jesus,
and for your reminder to always serve the Lord and
always forgive!*

Contents

Acknowledgments

I WOULD LIKE TO thank everyone who helped me from when I began writing this book until its publication.

First, I would like to thank Dr. Ruth Mills-Robbins and Mr. Eric Twisselmann, who read my very first chapter and encouraged me to continue the project. Also, I would like to thank my colleagues, Dr. Emilio Kariuki and Dr. Rosemary Mbogo, who read my first draft and gave me constructive feedback concerning African cultural issues addressed in the book.

When the manuscript was complete, Karen Myers read it and gave me constructive feedback on American issues that are addressed in the book. Also, Jessica Brown used her writing skills to edit the manuscript before it was sent to the publisher.

May I also appreciate everyone whose name is mentioned in the book. It is because of your friendship that my life has been transformed.

But I would not have had the experiences I am sharing if Biola University had not given me a scholarship when I came to study in 2007. Additionally, I would like to thank Biola for the quality education that has contributed to my transformation.

Finally, thank you my dear wife, Salome. Our twenty-seven years of companionship and partnership in ministry have transformed me more than any other human

Acknowledgments

relationship. And our children, Pélagie, Jean Paul, Jean Pierre and Gentille, too have helped me see the world from a new perspective!

Foreword

THIS WORK DEALS WITH one of the great problems of human life. Students of human nature have always affirmed the truth of the old German proverb, "Ein mensch ist kein mensch"—"one human being is no human being" or "one human being is nobody." As the Christian God of the Bible entails Father, Son, and Spirit in eternal relations, so human persons, created in the image of God, are truly persons only in relation to other persons. But whether individual to individual, group to group, or nation to nation, we struggle to relate to those who are "other" to us.

Out of a background of personal experience in the violence of Africa especially the 1994 Rwandan genocide and many years in a ministry of reconciliation among victims of violence in many African countries, Dr. Faustin Ntamushobora powerfully addresses this issue utilizing the African philosophical and theological concept of *ubuntu* or "humanity." According to *ubuntu* the individual is part of a greater whole. "I" am joined to "the other" so much so that any devaluation of the "other" through humiliation or oppression is also my devaluation. I similarly participate in the exaltation of the other. The issue of forgiveness and its freeing power, as should be expected, is also prominent in the discussion as well as the means of personal transformation which enables a person to actually live with the "other" in the reality of *ubuntu*.

Dr. Ntamushobora validly grounds this African principle of humanity in the biblical picture of the body of Christ in which each member is not only a part of the whole but "members one of another" (Rom. 12:5). His discussion of forgiveness is particularly touching coming out of his mother's amazing action which powerfully influenced him and his ministry. He thoughtfully and compellingly explains how the offender and the victim can find reconciliation at the Cross of Christ.

It was my privilege to get acquainted with Dr. Ntamushobora as one of the advisor's on the doctoral committee. As the main concepts of this book reflect his dissertation studies they were naturally the topics of our discussions. Whether I added anything to him is his to say, but for me I was freshly impacted by these truths perhaps as never before. I was hearing them through a person who, because of the life journey he had walked with God, was filled with these biblical concepts. Now they are a greater part of me.

Although the reader of this book may never have the privilege of talking with its author personally, the book is in many ways the story of a man whom God led through various experiences and diverse contexts to give himself to helping people understand and live a truly human life of unity with diversity. Through the interesting writing style, combining teaching and testimony, one is impacted as though listening to the heart of this man of God.

Robert L. Saucy
Distinguished Professor of Theology,
Talbot School of Theology, Biola University

Introduction

WHEN I MOVED TO Kenya in 1995 with my family for my master's program, I took an undergraduate course on communication and culture. In the class, my professor told us a story about a Maasai man and his wife who came to Nairobi for the first time. They traveled from Kajiado, about a hundred miles away, to visit their son who was studying at the Daystar campus. Next to the Daystar campus was a roundabout that was tricky to cross. The man and his wife had seen cars before, but they were not accustomed to the heavy traffic and careless driving in Nairobi. After the son crossed the road, he waited for his parents, who were both wearing *shukas*, an African cloth about the size of a bed sheet. As the man began to cross the road, his wife was seized with fear that her husband would be hit by a quickly approaching car. In the frenzy of the moment, she grasped for her husband—only to pull on his *shuka*. As a result, the wife remained with the *shuka* in hand as the husband ran across the road naked.

If someone can go through culture shock in his native country, how much more shock will he experience when he is in a foreign country? We all go through different experiences when we encounter different people or when we visit different places. Although these experiences may seem undesirable, they can lead to our transformation.

In this book, I am writing about my personal transformation through my encounters with people of different races, tribes, worldviews, and experiences, and how God has used these encounters to transform my life into the image of Christ. The "different other" in this book means someone from a different race, tribe, or worldview perspective. In the African context, the "other" implies inclusion. It is the other person who comes to extend my being so that I may be able to truly say, "I am because we are." It is the other person whose interaction with me increases my wisdom, for as the Akan people in Ghana say, "Wisdom is like a baobab tree; no one individual can embrace it." This concept of the other is different from the Western concept as coined by Gayatri Spivak, which is "a relationship created by imperial discourse to connote an abstract and generalized but more symbolic representation of empire's 'other.'"[1] "Othering" in the Western context denotes some exclusion. Historically, it has also denoted an idea of an superior-inferior relationship and the relationship between the colonizer and the colonized.

In this book, I am also drawing from the findings of my doctoral dissertation research. This research indicated that for the Africans I interviewed, transformation was "through the other and for the other." Using this principle, I apply it to the different other, which then corroborates the philosophy of *ubuntu* that is at the heart of my endeavor for racial and tribal reconciliation. *Ubuntu* is an African term that means "humanness" and that calls us to consider others as humans as opposed to dehumanizing them.

In this book, I will share selected intercultural experiences related to the theme of transformation through the different other in some of the countries I have lived in. Particularly, I am narrating the frustration and joy that I experienced through my encounters with "the different other" during the five years of study at Biola University in California. Of these five years, I spent four years serving as an

1. Ashcoft, Griffitths, and Tiffin, *Post-Colonial Studies*, 156.

adjunct professor at Biola. During this time, I had the privilege of interacting with American faculty, staff, and students.

While in the States, I founded a nonprofit organization, Transformational Leadership in Africa (TLAfrica, Inc.), which trains leaders in five African countries in East Africa. The US board of directors and staff are men and women of Caucasian, African American, Chinese, Korean, and Bahamian descent. I will be drawing from this part of my life too, narrating my challenging yet transformative cross-cultural leadership experiences with the US board and staff of TLAfrica, Inc.

For those who do not know me, I am a Rwandan Christian leader who witnessed and survived the 1994 genocide. Born in the Democratic Republic of Congo, I served in Kenya for twelve years before my family and I went to the States for my doctoral studies at Biola. While in Kenya, I served as Africa director for African Leadership And Reconciliation Ministries (ALARM, Inc.), a ministry that operates in eight countries in East Africa.

The purpose of this book is threefold. First, it prepares Americans to be vessels of God for the transformation of those who come to their country from other countries and from different worldviews. In so doing, the book prepares both Americans and those who move to or visit the States for a long period of time to practice true rendezvous of giving and receiving, which will transform two culturally different people into the image of Christ.

Second, this rendezvous offers practical, Christ-centered solutions for racial issues that lurk in the States, and indeed, all countries of the world.

Third, this book sets forth ideas at the core for my vision for a Christian university in Rwanda. This book proposes an educational paradigm of interracial reconciliation based on the African philosophy of *ubuntu* (a person discovering his or her fullness in community) and the concept of transformation through the different other. This philosophy of *ubuntu* is one of the three pillars of my vision for Thousand Hills International University, a Christian university we are planning to establish in Rwanda to train Rwandans with a transformational curriculum integrating faith and learning, empowering the graduates to bring holistic transformation in their communities. The three pillars of this university are:

1) a curriculum that is relevant and contextualized—a curriculum that speaks to the soul of Rwandans and addresses their needs;

2) a philosophy of *ubuntu*, thus allowing Rwandans to see each other as people with the same ancestor, Kanyarwanda, using their differences to build each other and their nation, and considering each other as one's extension;

3) a vision that prepares Rwandans to be a part of God's plan for the Great Commission in Africa and the world, especially in this time when Sub-Sahara Africa has become a center of gravity for Christianity on the globe.

Chapter 1 of this book deals with the human heart. I begin by explaining that the problem among people of different races and worldviews is not primarily their differences—but rather the human heart. I use my experiences in life and ministry in Africa to explain how the heart can be deceitful beyond measure. But I also show that the heart can immeasurably bless: the "different other" can cause beautiful growth. In this case, instead of the other constituting exclusion, the other becomes a continuation of myself—an inclusion that

makes "I" and "you" a community of two different interdependent hearts capable of sharpening each other.

In chapter 2 I speak about gaps created by differences
in race or tribe. In this chapter, I admit that although the different other is not the primary problem of exclusion, differences in worldview, color, and tribe could contribute to such
a problem. I do so using selected experiences in my five-year
life in the States when I was a doctoral student at Biola.

After the two chapters that highlight my experiences
of transformation through the different other, I establish a
theoretical foundation for these experiences in chapter 3. I
suggest that the solution to the exclusionary attitude (the
"us" versus "them" perspective) is the use of the African
philosophy of *ubuntu* and its theological significance that
brings unity in diversity.

In chapter 4, the book moves from experience and
theory to practice. This chapter answers the question, "How
does transformation through the different other happen?"
Here, I use the findings of my doctoral research, which reveal the principle that the different other leads to a perspective transformation that is useful to the individual and the
community.

Finally, the book concludes with a call for a rendezvous of giving and receiving, a concept which has the potential to enact change in daily life and in leadership among
people from different tribes, races, and worldviews so that
the church of Jesus Christ may practice Revelation 5:9 here
and now: "praising the lamb of God who was slain and with
whose blood he purchased men for God from every tribe
and language and people and nation." I invite Christians
from every tribe and race to rehearse the praise that we will
sing from every tongue and every tribe for the Lamb of God
who was slain for us and for our salvation.

1

The Problem of the Human Heart

ONE TIME, AFTER SPEAKING about the genocide in Rwanda
to an American audience, a gentleman approached me and
asked, "Why did Rwandans kill each other?" I paused and
told him, "They killed each other for the same reasons that
Americans kill each other." He insisted that the story of
Hutu and Tutsi was too savage for such a connection.

Referring to the book on *Historiography of Genocide*[1]
that I had previously read, I gave him the case of how Native
Americans were killed by Europeans and their descendants,
the holocaust of Jews by the Germans, the genocide of the
Herero and Namaqua people in Namibia by the Germans
early in the twentieth century, and the Bosnia genocide that
took place during the same period as the Rwandan genocide in the 1990s. I asked him, "Were all these Hutus and
Tutsis?" My intention was not to cause guilt, nor was it to
condone the genocide in Rwanda, but to bring my friend to
the understanding that it is not primarily about Hutu and
Tutsi, but the human heart.

1. Stone, *Historiography of Genocide.*

For example, it is true that Europeans have done evil things that continue to have consequences on the African continent. This is atrocious. Yet we must not overlook the fact that Africans themselves have inflicted the same evils on their fellow Africans. The genocide in Rwanda that killed almost a million people within a hundred days is one of such evils. People do not understand how people who speak the same language, have lived together for centuries, and have even intermarried could turn against each other. But that did not happen because they were Rwandans; it happened because the murderers did not have loving hearts. Far from pointing the finger to race and ethnic belonging, we need to know that "the heart is deceitful above all things and beyond cure" (Jer 17:9).

The issue of man's heart being evil is not new for me. I have seen this many times in my life, and it is even expressed in my name. John Mbiti explains, "In African societies, a name generally describes some personality or characteristics of someone,"[2] and my name, Ntamushobora, means "no one can please the world." There is also a story with my name. One day, my dad and I were traveling together to check on our cows, which were being kept with a friend's large herd in Bikaniro, eastern Congo. Because my dad was mentoring me, he asked me to go with him. On the way, he used the journey to tell me why he called me Ntamushobora.

He told me about two of his friends who would always come to our home every time my dad had banana beer, and my dad would voluntarily give them some beer to drink. But instead of appreciating him, one day they went to falsely accuse him to Mwami, which is the title for the king. They said my dad was planning to influence other people in the village to rebel against Mwami. My dad was arrested and

2. Mbiti, *Concepts of God in Africa*, 26.

put in jail, but after the investigation Mwami learned it was a false accusation, that my dad was a good man who was loyal to Mwami. So my dad told me, "Son, that is why when you were born I called you Ntamushobora, for 'no-one can please the world.'"

The meaning of my name came powerfully to my mind after I became a Christian. After I received God's amazing and unconditional love and repented of my sins and put my faith in Jesus, I said to myself, "I agree with my dad that it is difficult to please the world, but I will not tire of doing good for others, even if they do not reciprocate, for when I do good, it is unto the Lord." This philosophy of doing good to every person, even to the enemy, not only found its foundation in the grace that God has demonstrated to me by forgiving my sins and putting his word in my heart, but it also made its pathway in my mum's testimony when she forgave those who had killed her three children in the same week. (In fact, I was also to die with them, but I found grace before God and survived).

Let me tell you how this happened. I was born into a family that did not know the Lord. My dad was a traditional priest. He used to sacrifice to ancestors. We were eight children, and I was the seventh child. For reasons I do not know, my dad had chosen me to be his heir in sacrificing to ancestors. From time to time my dad would slaughter a goat, and I was the one to lay hands upon it—a sign of dedicating the goat to our ancestors—before it was slaughtered. After slaughtering the goat, we would roast some of the meat and put it in small huts behind our house. Some other boys and I would wait for my dad to leave, so that we could sneak into the huts and eat the meat. When my dad found the meat gone, he would say, "Son, the ancestors have eaten the meat." I kept quiet so that he would not beat me up.

But my dad did not live long. He became sick, and when he worsened, my mum called other traditional priests to sacrifice a bull for the healing of my dad. Despite the sacrifice, my dad passed away. A year after my dad passed away, when some missionaries came to the village and preached the gospel to my mum, she understood that it is not the ancestors who are between man and God, but Jesus Christ. She was open to biblical teaching because the ancestors had not healed her husband despite the sacrifice of a bull! So, my mum accepted Christ, and she did her best to raise me in the ways of the Lord.

However, I did not have a personal relationship with the Lord. There was tension between knowledge of the Bible in my head and rebellion against surrendering myself to the will of God in my heart. I knew many Bible verses, but they remained only in my mind; they never sunk down to the heart. And I was a good hypocrite. I would go out with young men in the evening and smoke and drink banana beer, but I would not miss my Sunday school. No one knew these hidden things. Everybody in the village thought that Ntamushobora was a good boy. I was a good singer in the choir despite the fact that my heart was far from the Lord. I even registered as a candidate for water baptism.

On the day of baptism, the preacher spoke from 2 Corinthians 5:17: "When one is in Christ he is a new creation; the old is gone, behold everything is new." The speaker was using two pieces of wood to illustrate the old and the new creation. When I examined my life, I found that although I was going to be baptized, I was still an old creation. This truth shook me to the core. When the preacher made the altar call, I repented for my sins and surrendered my life to Christ. That was on December 19, 1979—when my whole life changed. I felt great joy and peace.

As I said earlier, after my dad passed away in 1968, the following year my mum became a Christian. In those years, the people of the village hated our family. My dad was a wealthy man; we had a large portion of land and a large banana plantation. The fact that my mum had four boys and two girls all of good conduct brought jealousy among other women. My older brother was a teacher in a Baptist primary school, which was a high position in the village. Then, in 1970, a year after my mum became a Christian, four of us in our family were given poison by people in the village. My younger brother, my older brother, my older sister and I were poisoned.

Once we were poisoned, we all became ill. We were given herb medicine to vomit the poison, but it did not work for my siblings. For reasons I do not know, even with herb medicine they could not vomit the poison. During our time of sickness, what made my mum even more sad was not just the death of her children, but their death without leaving grandchildren. My older brother was engaged, and so was my older sister. We had already taken two cows for my older sister's dowry; all that remained was the marriage ceremony. As an African, my mum wished that my older brother and sister had left a child behind before their death! But she could not redeem the situation.

On a Monday, my young brother passed away and was buried the same day. On Wednesday of the same week, my older brother passed away and was buried the same day too. I heard about the news of the death of my two brothers, but I was not able to attend their funeral, for I was in a critical condition, weakened by vomiting. On Friday of the same week my older sister passed away. I was the one who survived, maybe to be able to tell this story.

That Friday, during the burial ceremony of my sister, I listened to my mum ask the elders to allow her say something before the burial of my sister's body. Generally speaking, women do not speak at funerals in Africa. But because her husband was no longer living and because she had lost three children the same week, the elders allowed her to speak.

My mum said, "I know those who have killed my children, and I have a solution for them." She paused. Everyone came closer to hear this solution. I can remember my mum touching her head with her two hands joined together. Her voice was exhausted, her eyes red, for she had not slept for many days. She said, "Last year I accepted Christ who died on the cross where I was to die. But Christ forgave my sins." She paused again, and everyone became silent. My mum said, "For the sake of Christ, I forgive those who have killed my children."

People murmured because they could not believe it! The elders appreciated my mum and said to leave everything to God who is the supreme judge. People thought that my mum would be depressed, but God gave her peace.

My mum is ninety as I write this book, but her story of forgiveness has molded me. Every time we meet, my mum has two messages for me. The first is, "Son, always remember the Lord who saved you from death when your three siblings died, and always serve him." The second message is, "Son, you remember how I forgave those who killed your three siblings; always forgive!"

But my survival after my three siblings died was not my only lesson to learn about reconciliation. God—or the "Great Other" as I call him—is amazing! To prepare me for more reconciliation ministry, God allowed me and my family to experience the horror of the genocide, a time of spiritual warfare that I had never experienced in life.

It is easy to read books about genocide, but it is far different from the reality that was lived during that time.

What I believe is that Satan works in man's heart to kill, steal, and destroy. The genocide was a time when Satan was in control of the land and people of Rwanda. People had lost their sense of *ubuntu*—humanness—that we will speak about later in this book. One cannot understand, humanly speaking, how people can kill innocent children! Again, such actions show how far man's heart, if used by Satan, can go.

I remember how when I went to the Eastern Mennonite University in 2004 for a course on Trauma Awareness and Recovery, we were told to bring an instrument that constituted our hope during our time of horror. I took the course with people from different religious beliefs. Among them were Muslims, Jews, and Hindus. These were people who had either experienced the events of September 11 in the USA or had lost their relatives that day. For me, I carried my old Kinyarwanda Bible. For the twenty-six days that my family spent hidden under the bed for fear of being killed, God sustained our hearts through the reading of Psalms. One of my favorite was Psalm 46, especially verses 1, 2, and 11:

> [1]God is our refuge and our strength,
>   an ever-present help in trouble.
> [2]Therefore we will not fear, though the earth give way
>   and the mountain fall into the heart of the sea,
> though its waters roar and foam and the mountains quake
>   with their surging.
> [11]The LORD Almighty is with us;
>   the God of Jacob is our fortress.

This experience played a part in changing my heart into the image of Christ. As a survivor, I was not better than those who lost their lives during the genocide. Rather, Rwandans who live today and who were in Rwanda during the genocide should know that God spared their lives for a purpose: to tell what happened and to be used of God for a greater purpose of preaching the gospel of reconciliation with God, self, and the other. That is what I saw God doing through me after the genocide. For five years I served as director of African Leadership And Reconciliation Ministries (ALARM, Inc.), training leaders in matters of reconciliation in Burundi, Eastern Congo, Kenya, Rwanda, Southern Sudan, Uganda, Tanzania, and Zambia. Most of these countries went through terrible times of divisions and wars and needed reconciliation.

The war in Sudan, which ended in 2005 with the comprehensive peace agreement between the Sudan People's Liberation (SPL) and the Khartoum government, had lasted more than twenty years. Uganda was suffering from the atrocities that the Lord's Resistance Army was afflicting upon people in Northern Uganda. Burundi had gone through civil war since October 1993 when the elected president Merchior Ndadaye was assassinated.

In Congo, the ousted dictator Mobutu killed thousands of innocent civilians. Since the war in Congo began in 1997, Eastern Congo has never been at peace. Furthermore, it is heart-breaking that the international community has not acknowledges the suffering that women in Congo have gone through. These women are not politicians, nor are they soldiers; they are simple agricultural villagers who have fallen victims of those who are fighting. Though these soldiers use politics as their motivation, in truth they are fighting for the rich minerals and other resources in Eastern Congo. The soldiers, in addition to robbing the country, are raping these innocent women. Some of the women have been infected with HIV/AIDS, and others have continued to suffer from physical and emotional wounds. In *National Geographic*, Draper narrates the story of a Congolese lady who was a victim of the militia. He writes,

> A woman named Faida weeps quietly as she recalls what happened to her a year ago. She is petite, with fatigued eyes and a voice just above a whisper. In her hands is a letter from her husband, demanding that she leaves their house because he feared she might have contracted HIV from the man who raped her.[3]

Pause and reflect on the pain of this woman. Faida and the Congolese are suffering because of the resources in their country. People have lost their relatives; women are raped every day. Man's heart is indeed deceitful.

One of my difficult but powerful ministries was to lead people suffering from great pain like Faida into trauma healing. When I was working with ALARM, Inc. we would gather small groups of people who had gone through traumatic events and we would help them release their pain to the cross of Jesus. We would gather in a quiet place for three days, and we would use the Gospel of Mark to explain the journey of Christ. At the climax of the journey was the cross of Jesus, which we literally placed in our midst. Then we would explain the importance of the cross, God's forgiveness and the importance of forgiveness in the believer's life. We the facilitators would take the lead and share our pain; then we would move close to the cross to bring our pain to Jesus. We would invite participants to come closer and pray for us. This step would open the relationship of trust so that participants who were led by the Spirit to share would do so too. Then, we would pray a prayer of healing for their hearts.

I remember a trauma healing retreat that we organized at Tigoni, Limuru, in Kenya in 2004. A lady called Chantale shared the story of the murder of her relatives. She had lost nineteen relatives in the war in Bunia between

3. Draper, *National Geographic*, 109.

the Hima and Lendu. After talking for forty-five minutes, she was sweating. Also, her language had changed; she was speaking in a whisper. She looked exhausted, but she did not want to stop before she finished. She wanted to make sure she brought all her pain to the cross of Jesus. Finally, she said, "I, I . . . forgive!" She breathed a deep sigh. As I looked at her, her face immediately changed. She smiled at us and she said, "I have released all my burdens to Christ; now I am free; I am no longer a slave of revenge and bitterness." Forgiveness has liberating power!

Yes, man's heart is deceitful. Not just in Congo and Rwanda—even in Kenya, man's heart is deceitful. I remember when I went to Kenya in 1995, Kenyans could not understand how Rwandans killed each other. But the same thing happened in Kenya in December 2007. Kenyans who had been living together and who had intermarried killed each other just as Rwandans had done thirteen years before.

I remember when my wife and I went to Kenya in the summer of 2008 and spoke at our former church, Limuru Town Baptist Church. After the worship service, Christians from a sister church called Word of Faith, who knew me and my ministry of reconciliation brought me a woman whose whole body had been burnt during the Kenya tribal clashes. They said, "Pastor Faustin, please say something to this woman." What a test! I was filled with compassion for this woman, but I did not know what to say. I paused and looked at her. Suddenly, I felt compelled to share the story of my mum and how she forgave those who had killed her three children in the same week. Indeed, I did share the story. The woman listened attentively. At the end I said, "Can we pray?" She responded, "Yes, we can pray," and she smiled.

After we had prayed, those who had brought the woman told me in her presence that this was the first time she had smiled since she had been burnt. The woman confessed the same and said, "You smile when your heart is warm; but nothing so far had made my heart warm. But after this pastor shared his mum's story and made me understand that forgiveness is a miracle the Holy Spirit brings when we forgive, I felt some change in my heart. That is why I smiled."

At times it has been tremendously difficult for me to say something to those hurting. Sometimes I have wept with those who are weeping. I know it is against the counseling principles that I learned in a Western curriculum, but as an African I have cried with those who are hurting, and it has helped me and it has helped those in pain.

I remember in 2005 when I was training Sudanese refugee pastors in Adjumani in Northern Uganda. I spent a week training them in matters of reconciliation, preparing them to return to Sudan and preach unity and reconciliation after the Comprehensive Peace Agreement was signed. Just the day before I was to leave, as I was teaching about the ministry of trauma healing, one pastor got a phone call. He went out to answer the phone. A few moments later, we all heard him crying. I stopped teaching, and two pastors went to help him. They spoke in the Kakwa language (one of the local Southern Sudanese languages), and the two pastors cried with him. As a whole class, we went out and asked what had happened. The Lord's Resistance Army had abducted the firstborn son of the pastor who had received the call. When we all heard the news, we all cried and prayed together, inviting God to be "Emmanuel" with the boy who had been abducted. We claimed protection and release of the boy in the name of Jesus. We asked our ministry staff and partners to pray for the situation. I decided to postpone my trip back to Nairobi to spend more time with the family, but soon I had return to Nairobi. A week later, I received the news that Joseph Kony, the leader of the Lord's Resistance Army, and his people had bitten the young boy and released him in the forest saying, "Let's leave him to die in the forest." The boy wandered through the forest for many days until finally finding his way to the village. When we heard this, we praised God for the protection of the young boy.

Even in the midst of pain caused by the deceitfulness of the human heart, there is good news for the healing of this heart, and this healing comes from the one who created the heart. As C. S. Lewis puts it:

> What Satan put into the heads of our ancestors was the idea that they could "be like gods"—could set up on their own as if they had created themselves—be their own masters—invent some sort of happiness for themselves outside God, apart from God. . . . The reason why it can never succeed is this: God made us: invented us as a man invents an engine. A car is made to run on gasoline, and it would not run properly on anything else. Now God designed the human marching to run on Himself. He Himself is the fuel our spirits were designed to burn or the food our spirits were designed to feed on. There is no other. That is the key to history. Terrific energy is expended—civilizations are build up—excellent institutions devised; but each time something goes wrong. . . . In fact the machine conks. They are trying to run it on the wrong juice.[4]

God, the creator of man, is able to transform man's heart, and he does it in a loving way that you and I cannot fathom. This love was expressed by God sending his son, Jesus Christ, to die on the cross for the forgiveness of our sin. Those who are forgiven are saved from the wrath of God and are given an eternal gift of everlasting life, such as the one I was given when I responded to the message of 2 Corinthians 5:17 on December 19, 1979. My heart was

4. Lewis, *Mere Christianity*, 39.

changed. The same word of God that changed me continues to change many others who accept that they are sinners and need a Savior, irrespective of their color and origin.

In fact, as you read this book, you will be surprised that the most enjoyable and transformative moments of seeing lives changed took place as I was ministering with people of another race. One such moment was when my wife, Salome, and I were conducting a marriage conference. We were in Malindi, Kenya, near the Indian Ocean in 2005 with Warren and Sue, from Oklahoma State. I was then the Africa director of ALARM, Inc., and Warren and Sue were our main partners in marriage conferences. They had a background in Campus Crusade, and so evangelism was part of their training; they both knew how to integrate evangelism in every aspect of teaching. They did not assume that everyone was a Christian, but gave a chance for people to respond to the message of salvation.

Warren and Sue were facilitating a marriage session with forty couples. One of these couples, Kenneth and Beatrice, were attending the conference. Kenneth was not a Christian, but his wife Beatrice had requested him to attend the conference with her. Kenneth liked the teaching about marriage because it addressed a problem he was facing with his wife. But a time came when Warren introduced the gospel message, explaining that it is only through God's Holy Spirit that the participants could carry out the concepts in the marriage teaching. Warren explained that the Holy Spirit dwells only in the hearts of those whose sins have been forgiven through the washing of the blood of Jesus. Then Warren, limited in his cultural background as an American, stopped and took his seat.

From the participants' body language and eye contact, I immediately felt that the Holy Spirit was moving among participants. Then I stood up and continued where Warren had stopped. I summarized the teaching of Warren and Sue, and I made an altar call, encouraging people to put their faith in Christ as their Savior and Lord.

As I was asking people to come to surrender their lives to Christ, I noticed Beatrice crying. I also saw her holding the hands of her husband. As she explained later, she was crying because her husband had just whispered to her that he was ready to accept the gift of salvation. I moved close to Beatrice and her husband and asked them, "Is there something the Holy Spirit is telling you to do?" Beatrice did not say anything but stood up and brought me her husband, holding his hands in hers, crying tears of joy. When I asked Kenneth, "Why are you coming forward?" he said, "I need the gift of salvation today." I led him to accept Christ as Savior and Lord. Since then Beatrice and her husband have been great friends to me, my wife, Warren, and Sue.

Here is an example of the power of the Word of God piercing someone's heart through the power of the Holy Spirit. The Word of God has power to transform and to heal. The Word of God transcends cultures for three reasons:

- It is this Word that has the power to transform the deceptive heart and make it right before God.

- It is this Word that delivers us from our tendency to cling to our traditional cultural values and behaviors.

- It is this Word that removes the blindness that makes us see "the other" only as a label: as Hutu, Tutsi, black, white, colonizer, uncivilized, or other simplistic categories.

In his book *Life with God: Reading the Bible for Spiritual Transformation*, Richard J. Foster[5] writes about the transforming power of the Word of God. Foster invites

5. Foster, *Life with God*, 7.

believers into a deeper and more authentic life with God, reminding us that biblical knowledge should lead us to greater appropriation of God's love and a greater love for God, others, and ourselves. The author reminds us that the Bible is not a tool for sharpening religious competence, but a living and active sword for cleaving our double-minded thoughts and motives, exposing and transforming the content of our hearts.[6] Unfortunately, this is not the case for the church in Africa, or for perhaps much of the world. Many discipleship programs give information but do not provide a way for the information to sink down to the heart and generate change. Foster suggests that we should read the Bible with the whole heart, not just the mind. Instead of perceiving the Bible only as a guidebook to religious life, we can understand it as a collection of stories that testify to one grand story of a personal God in pursuit of relationship with human beings.[7]

As I write this book, I am thinking about the way Africans can partner with Westerners to bring transformation among their people. Africans are naturally religious. For us Africans, "religion is like the skin that you carry along with you wherever you go, not like the cloth that you wear now and discard the next moment"[8] That is why it becomes easier for us to read the Bible with the heart. On the other side, Westerners are more interested, generally speaking, in reading the Bible with the mind. This is something inherited from Enlightenment thought, encapsulated in Descartes' edict, "I think, therefore I am." So together, Africans and Americans can enrich each other harmoniously—just like a guitar with several chords, some people sing bass and others tenor! Personally, most of my greatest mentors and key

6. Ibid., 75.

7. Ibid, 101

8. King, "Under the Mango Tree," 150.

partners have been Americans. I have learned from them as they have learned from me. Through this mutual enrichment, believers from both sides of the ocean can bless each other with the Word of God and through interaction with each other. This cross-cultural encounter can help remove or reduce our myopia so that we may see each other as true children of God.

The Word of God is supracultural: it transcends cultures. This was demonstrated during a marriage conference that Transformational Leadership in Africa, Inc. (TLAfrica) organized in Ruhengeri, Rwanda, in July 2009.

I invited my friend, Pastor Edward Morsey from California, to teach at the conference. I knew Ed was a fine teacher of the Word because I had been learning from him for two years. At first, Ed wasn't ready to accept the invitation. First, he questioned the idea of contextualization, asking me how relevant his teaching would be to African couples. Second, he questioned the expense of the trip: wouldn't it be better just to give the money to a local ministry?

Through discussion, we agreed that his teaching would be relevant because he would not be teaching culture, but the Word of God, which transcends cultures. Secondly, I told him that the message of a visitor has more power than the message of the local person, if delivered in a relevant way. Finally, the Spirit of the Living God convinced Ed, and he accepted the invitation. I appreciated Ed's wife, Karen, for approving Ed's trip to Africa, for she would be alone for about two weeks, not knowing what was going to happen to her husband!

Ed became, as Africans say, "a visitor who brought rain with him"—meaning, he brought blessings. During the three-day conference for twenty-two pastors and their wives, Pastor Ed taught about marriage from a biblical perspective; the Word of God could speak for itself. When we concluded the conference on Saturday, Ed summarized the teaching and sat down. I stood up and, looking at the faces of pastors and their wives, felt the Spirit at work in our hearts.

I said, "We have been learning under the Holy Spirit through Pastor Ed for three days, and the Word of God has done some amazing work in our lives. Is there someone who would like to share his or her experience of what it has meant to be here?" Then I kept quiet.

One man stood up and said to us, "Brethren, I would like to confess before my wife, you and God, that I have been mistreating my wife. I was following the Rwandan culture of being a husband instead of applying what the Word of God says about being a husband." He asked his wife to forgive him, but at that moment, his wife could not look at him. Then three other men stood up with similar confessions. This was the first time I saw Rwandan men apologizing to their wives in public!

What did I do? I called these four men and their wives to come forward. I also called for three elders among the pastors and asked them to stand behind the couples confessing to each other, just for encouragement. I spoke to the ladies, "You have heard the confession of your husbands. Do you accept their apologies?" They all responded, "Yes," and immediately their faces changed. I asked the women to hug their husbands as sign of their forgiveness. They all did so with great joy. All the people began to sing songs of praise. As the couples returned to their seats, the other pastors hugged the four men who had apologized, and all the women hugged the four wives. It was a time of great joy for us who had witnessed the confessions.

A year later, we had a follow-up conference in Kampala, Uganda, and again I invited Pastor Ed to travel with me. We invited one of the couples whose husband had confessed to his wife. In a personal conversation, I asked the man, "What did you feel after you apologized to your wife in public last year?" He said, "That it was liberating for me; it was like a burden fell down from my head. I felt relieved." It is true; forgiveness has liberating power, as we can see in this next experience.

In July 2009, Living Word Fellowship Church from Houston, Texas, and TLAfrica partnered to facilitate a conference in Ruhengeri, Rwanda, for two hundred pastors from Rwanda, Burundi, Congo, and Uganda. On the third day of the conference, Pastor Cannings taught the pastors about leadership; then it was my time to teach. After a short song, I prayed and invited the Holy Spirit of the Living God to minister to us in a special way.

I introduced the topic of forgiveness, and stated that forgiveness is a liberating power for both the offender and the offended. I told the story of my mum and how she forgave those who had killed her three children. I read Ephesians 4:31–32. But before I finished teaching, I heard a voice encouraging me to make an altar call. My discernment confirmed that it was the voice of the Holy Spirit, but I was afraid of making an altar call for pastors and bishops. But I had to obey anyway! I made the altar call.

Forty pastors came to kneel down, and Pastor Cannings prayed for them. They went back to their seats—but one pastor remained kneeling down, crying.

As we were singing, he stood and whispered to me, "Pastor Faustin, it is not enough for me. I would like to make a public confession." I asked everyone to sit and invited him to speak. He said, "This message came specifically to me. Let me ask my bishop to stand up." His bishop stood up. "I have made this man's life difficult just because he is from a different tribe." With tears, he cried, "Bishop, please forgive me. I ask you all to pray that the Lord may forgive me and liberate me from my ethnic spirit." The bishop came forward, and hugged him. They both cried tears of joy, and a group of pastors came to pray for them. It was a time of true joy, which some participants had never experienced before.

In the summer of 2011, Pastor Cannings and I went back to Rwanda for the graduation of the two pastors and others who had attended our leadership training. We were delighted to see the two pastors fellowshipping together.

With the help of the Holy Spirit and the transforming Word of God, we also participate in God's healing through self-disclosure.

Self-disclosure, though, is not an easy thing. F. R. Verderber explains that people do not describe their feelings, or do not disclose, as a result of one of the three assumptions:

- "First, people may believe that if they really tell their feelings they would reveal too much about themselves and so become vulnerable."

- "Second, people believe that their feelings will in some way hurt other people."

- "Finally, people may feel guilty about the feelings they have."[9]

I have experienced these assumptions at work. When I was Africa director of ALARM and after my training for Trauma Awareness and Recovery, we used to organize trauma healing retreats for people from Rwanda, Burundi, Eastern Congo, and Sudan who had suffered emotional pain caused by wars in their nations. During these retreats, some participants would disclose; they would share the agonies within their hearts and bring them to the cross of

9. Verderber, *Communicate!*, 72–73.

Jesus. But others would go through the three days of the retreat without sharing.

When people relate, we do so at different levels. Some of the deeper levels of communication facilitate self-disclosure, but if we cannot reach such depth, how can we experience the healing self-disclose brings? W. C. Icenogle[10] explains that in dyadic or group communication there are five levels of communication:

1. Level one is cliché conversation. This represents the least willingness to share myself with others. This is conversation that avoids engagement. I remember the first time I met my wife Salome in high school; our first conversation consisted of clichés, just quick hellos in the hallway.

2. Level two is about reporting the facts. This represents a minimal sharing of myself—a sharing of objective knowledge. After Salome and I spent a year together at the same college, we began sharing basic information about ourselves.

3. Level three is that of sharing ideas and opinions. This represents giving more of the individual and unique self. This demands more risk-taking, for the other person has the potential to reject my idea or opinion. I remember Salome taking the risk to share with me what she thought about my relationship with another friend of hers. She did not mean to influence me to marry her, but she was telling me the truth as a sister in the Lord. At first, I didn't welcome her observation, but later on I realized she was right and apologized to her.

4. Level four is about sharing one's feelings, values, and emotions. These words represent one's personal self.

10. Icenogle, *Biblical Foundations*, 76–77.

At this level, one is now speaking from a more hidden part of his or her being. This is the level when I told Salome that I loved her. We first shared our feelings through letters, but the time came when I visited her at her village, met her relatives and opened my heart to her when I said, "I love you."

5. Level five is about confessional sharing. This represents peak communication. These are the experiences and feelings one may not ever share with another. There are many things I could not share with Salome before we got married. Even after marriage it took us time to disclose everything to one another.

If our sharing about pains and hurts caused by the other cannot reach Icenogle's fourth level of disclosure (feelings, values, and emotions), then we either are playing some political game or we are not ready to share intimately with the other. All in all, we must understand that the heart is sensitive. Sometimes, one may trust when the other is not ready to. Without reaching the deep levels of communication, fellowship may take place, but true transformation may be hindered. As believers come together to study the Word, fellowship, worship, and pray together, they bring their intellect as well as emotion. Unless the two are engaged, how can our wills truly be touched?

In a community, people have all sorts of emotions: fear of failing when asked a question, shame if one fails to answer a question during discussion, guilt of forgetting what one knows, pride resulting from knowing more than others, an inferiority or superiority complex depending on the position of the person in the group. However, all these tensions are inescapable—and in truth, these tensions are actually triggers for our transformation. The honesty in sharing these emotions bring a deeper level of communication and thus self-disclosure. Within the context of help from Holy Spirit and light from the Word of God, we can begin to experience healing and transformation.

Only life can shape life. A human being has the capacity either to commune with the other or to consume the other. Does it depend on race and worldview? In part it does, but the root cause is sin in the human's heart. The bad news is that a human being can use his heart to hurt and even destroy the heart of his fellow human being. The good news is that this same heart, if transformed by the Great Other, can shape and even bring hope to the heart of the other.

The following chapter demonstrates how the deceitfulness of the human heart coupled with differences in race, tribe, and worldview can make the gap among different people wider, and thus make hearts all the more willing to consume each other. I invite you to hear the stories in the next chapter.

2

The Gap Between Us

CHAPTER 1 HAS DEMONSTRATED that differences in race, tribe and worldview are not the primary problems that divide people, but rather the heart is. This chapter seeks to acknowledge that race, tribe, and worldview differences can widen the gap among people's relationships, thus leading to exclusion, even for born-again Christians.

However, this chapter also acknowledges that these factors, far from separating people, could lead to mutual transformation. According to Ester, Braun, and Mohler, "Globalization is a matter of transaction between global transnational, national and sub-national players that simultaneously both serve the role of 'emitters' and 'receivers' of cross-border culture."[1] This is what I call a rendezvous of giving and receiving among people from different cultures. For this chapter, I am going to tell my story of living in the States and interacting with Americans. As I encountered others who were different from me, I learned how our differences could either alienate us or bring the chance for life-giving changes deep within us.

1. Ester, Braun, and Mohler, *Globalization*, 5.

JOURNEY TO LOS ANGELES

Saying goodbye is always difficult. I remember how difficult it was for me to say goodbye to my wife, Salome, and my four children. Pélagie had just begun university, the twins, Jean Paul and Jean Pierre, were in boarding high schools, and Gentille had just begun high school. The most challenging part was that I was leaving them without hope of joining me in the States. We did not have money for five air tickets; we did not even have the money to prove to the American Embassy that my family needed visas to join me.

But I had to go. For many years we had been praying, and we felt that God was prompting us to go to the States in order to study. Salome and I enjoyed serving our people in East Africa, and we felt God's calling for further training so that we could serve at a higher level.

Specifically, my desire for further training was motivated by my passion for writing materials that would be relevant and contextualized for the church in Africa. In his book *Western Education and Political Domination in Africa*, Magnus Bassey points out, "Education in Africa is still designed after Western models and paradigms that are not connected to life as it is in Africa."[2] He argues further that "African institutions, particularly African universities, still teach economics, political science, sociology, philosophy, geography, science, and so forth, as they are taught in Europe and America and with books imported from Europe and America."[3] No wonder graduates of such institutions are not connected to the life of the community! Bassey concludes, "What is taught in Africa has no direct relevance to the needs and circumstances of the people of Africa."[4]

2. Bassey, *Western Education*, 47.
3. Ibid.
4. Ibid.

Bassey's statement is not to be taken generally because I did my master's program at Daystar University, whose program was relevant to my ministry. Although the Western curriculum taught in schools in Africa has not, generally speaking, prepared Africans to transform their communities, some schools have done a good job of contextualizing their curriculum.

After graduating from Daystar University, I needed a school that would continue to shape my talents so that I would be more useful in God's kingdom. Although I did not know how my family would join me, we had faith that the Lord who had provided the scholarship for my doctoral studies would also provide for my family to join me. We also trusted the Lord for this because Salome and I had always modeled team leadership in our ministry, and being together was a training that could not be learned from a book in the library.

I do agree with my friends from the West that the practice of planning is important in life, and I challenge myself and my friends from Africa to make plans. But faith has its place too. Philip Jenkins writes about Christians believing in supernaturalism: "The critical idea is that God intervenes daily in everyday life"[5] is true of my faith. If we had depended on the amount of money we had before my journey to the States, I would not have left, and the Lord would not have opened the other doors of blessings: my family joining me, my wife studying for her master's, and new friends and partners in ministry. In addition, I would not have birthed the vision of TLAfrica or the beginning of a university in my country, Rwanda. I can speak of the difference between walking by sight and walking by faith as Adeyemo describes it:

5. Jenkins, *Next Christendom*, 77.

Transformation Through the Different Other

> Sight sees problems, vision sees potential,
> Sight sees plight of man, vision sees power of God,
> Sight sees barriers, vision sees bearings,
> Sight sees buffeting, vision sees blessings in disguise,
> Sight sees the natural, vision sees the supernatural,
> Sight sees the visible, vision sees the invisible,
> Sight sees the present, vision sees the past, present and
>   future,
> Sight sees danger only, vision sees opportunity as well,
> Sight sees dead ends, vision sees new beginnings,
> Sight sees the status quo, vision sees the possibility,
> Where sight gives up, vision goes on.[6]

The day I was to leave Kenya, we had a party at home and invited friends for a last prayer. Afterward, Jack, my former driver at ALARM, came to pick me up. We headed to the airport. How difficult it was when I had to hug everyone with the phrase, "*Kwaheri ya kuonana*"—goodbye and hope to see you.

I boarded the plane. In the morning I was in Amsterdam. It was not my first time to travel to the States, so I was able to navigate the airport at Amsterdam where I connected with the next plane to Los Angeles. I arrived at Los Angeles International Airport at 1:00 p.m.

Before I left Nairobi, my former mentor from Daystar University had connected me to Granada Heights Friends Church in what would be my new hometown of La Mirada, California. He had asked his close friend, Jim, to meet me at the airport. When I walked outside, Jim was nowhere to be seen. I waited for fifteen minutes and decided to call him from a phone booth.

When I called Jim, he advised me to wait, for he was still teaching a class. I waited for another forty-five minutes.

6. Quoted in an online comment to Bailey, "African Scholar Tokunboh Adeyemo Dies."

I was sleepy, battling jetlag. Finally, I saw him arrive. It was easy for him to identify me, for I was the only black person with luggage waiting to be picked up. Jim greeted me, and we began the journey to La Mirada. When he drove, he used the lane at the far end where few vehicles were. Out of curiosity I asked him why so few vehicles were in our lane. That was the first time I heard the words "carpool lane." He tried to explain it to me, but I was too sleepy to follow everything all he was saying. We finally reached home, where his wife Laurel welcomed me. With her hospitality, she made me feel right at home.

The next morning, both of them went to work early, so I had to find Biola University with a map Jim had drawn for me. I followed the map, but when I reached the traffic lights, I could not cross over because there was no crossing provided for pedestrians. The traffic light system was unfamiliar, certainly different from Nairobi's. I could not cross over for about twenty minutes. Then I saw a man arrive—he advanced me and touched a button on the electric pole. The sign for pedestrian crossing blinked and the guy crossed over, but it was too late for me to follow him. But I had learned what I needed to do! I touched the same electric pole hoping to produce some magic. I saw the pedestrian sign and crossed over quickly! I had just experienced one of my first culture shocks in La Mirada.

I arrived at Biola University. Someone showed me where the doctoral program office of Talbot School of Theology was located. There, I greeted Dr. Kevin Lawson, the program's director. He had come to Kenya a year before. I felt at home because we knew each other from Kenya.

Also that day, I met someone with whom I had been communicating for two years during my admission process: a woman named Tanya. To tell you the truth, I expected to see a man named Tanya, but to my surprise it was a lady. I was afraid to tell her that I thought she would be a man—and I'm not even sure why I thought she was. Perhaps it was because we do not have Tanyas in Africa, especially in the Francophone Africa where I grew up, or because American names don't have a prefix to show gender.

Tanya and Kevin are among the people have helped transform me in my journey in the States. Tanya is an exceptional administrator, born-again and filled with the Spirit of compassion and with the gift of serving. Kevin is a scholar and a pastor; his wife Patricia is welcoming and hospitable. She was the first person who invited me to have Thanksgiving dinner with her family.

I returned to my hosts' home that evening. Together we discussed where I would live next. They helped me find a room not far from Biola University, for I would be studying at the library late into the evenings. I moved to my new room, and for the next seventeen weeks and two days I only ate bread, eggs, and cups of tea. Jim and Laurel soon noticed that I was not eating well, so Laurel often invited me for lunch with their family after church. I bless my hosts and others for the role they played in my life during the absence of my family!

EXPERIENCES OF CULTURE SHOCK

What shocked me the most was the questions friends would ask me—questions that as an African I would take as inhospitable. In the African culture, a stranger is respected and welcomed, for a stranger brings blessings. It is rude to ask a visitor when he is going back before he has finished the mission that brought him there. But many Americans would ask me, "Faustin, will you go back home?" or "Faustin, when are you going back to Africa?" As an African, I saw the first question showing suspicion to whether I will go back or not. The second question indicated that the hosts are tired of living with the visitor. I would try to be polite and tell them, "Africa is my home. I came to study. When I finish I will go back" or "I will go back when I finish my studies or during summer time." Hopefully my fellow Americans and others will see that these two questions can hurt or confuse an African visitor. The better questions would be, "Welcome to our land, America. Do you have news of your family on the other side of the ocean?" or "We are happy to have you with us in our country; how long do you plan to spend with us?" There is such an important difference between the questions "How long will you be with us?" and "When are you going back?"

When I discussed these questions with Americans who understood intercultural issues, they made me understand that the Americans who ask such questions are innocent, which I understand. There is need, though, to learn from each other and know that these questions make Africans uncomfortable. Of course, I also made many mistakes asking the wrong questions, as we will see in the following pages. Ultimately, this way of thoughtful interaction shows how we can learn from each other and adapt in transformative ways.

The other serious culture shock I went through was the different way information is valued between Africans and Americans. Several times I shared what was going on in my life with friends—especially Christians, hoping they would listen to me and pray with me. They would of course listen to me and might have prayed for me, but what surprised me was to hear the things I shared with them coming from the mouths of many others who were not there when I shared. In Africa, if someone shares with you, it is with you and no one else. When I complained to my friends, asking them why others would share personal information, they asked me, "Did you tell them it was confidential?" I came to learn that if I share something in a small group, I should not be surprised if I hear it somewhere else.

When people visit a new place, they should not be surprised to find things done in a way different from the one they were familiar with. Lack of proper orientation could lead to serious mistakes. One of my mistakes was to buy a prepaid phone that I bought to make calls to Africa—for I badly needed to talk with my family. Surprisingly, I learned that I couldn't get this phone without a Social Security Number (SSN). What is a SSN? I asked many American friends how I could access a Social Security Number, but they had no idea.

I have learned that many Americans, generally speaking, are linear thinkers; their minds focus on something particular. For example, if someone does not need something right then, he doesn't bother knowing about it. Africans, though, are curious to learn everything, for wisdom says, "You might need it in the future, or someone from your family might need it." Another way of saying this is that Americans are outcome-oriented while Africans are relationship-oriented. But this does not excuse Americans from not being relationship-oriented or Africans from not being outcome-oriented. A balance is required for people on both sides of the ocean.

Coming back to my story of the mysterious SSN, after I was disappointed that nobody was helping me, I walked to a grocery store called Stater Brothers and bought a prepaid phone there. It turned out to be a very expensive phone. I would buy units for US $30 and use it all in one call!

But God intervened soon. I got a job through a man of God who trusted me even though I was new in the university, and that job led to me getting a Social Security Number. From there I was able to find an affordable cell phone plan.

I am sure there are many international students who have suffered like me in this country, and I hope that Americans who are reading this book will help newcomers so that the international students do not waste the little they have.

WHAT IS THIS F2 THAT ALMOST KILLED MY WIFE?

The coming of my family to the States was a miracle that God did, and it surprised many people. I remember sharing with my small group that I needed their prayers so that God could open a door for my family to join me. I told the group that we needed funds for three children and my wife. I remember one lady in our group saying, "Faustin, you need to be serious; how do you expect your family to join you in these situations?" I noticed that her eyes were seeing mountains while mine could see open opportunities. I told her, "That is how I have been operating all my life: putting God first in all I do and leaving mountains to him so that he may remove them to make my joy complete and to glorify himself." My life echoes an "Amen" to Sherwood Lingenfelter's assertion that "we must submit our values for achievement to the kingdom priority of trusting God for all outcomes, [for] since it is God's kingdom and God's Spirit who is moving in us, God is responsible for the results."[7]

I am glad that when my family finally arrived, my sister in the Lord came to share with me that my faith had impacted her. I myself am glad she spoke her doubt. I am sure there were several others who doubted as well. But the Lord used friends from both Africa and the United States to help bring my family to the States.

7. Lingenfelter, *Leading Cross-Culturally*, 49.

I would like to repeat that I believe in planning. I believe in saving. But in financial difficulties, I also believe that faith has some place to play. Otherwise, why should we pray, invoking God's power to come down and rivers of blessings to flow? Are they only spiritual rivers that flow? In truth, God's blessings come in a holistic way. Is he not the one feeding birds in the air? Why would he not open the door for his servant to live and enjoy fellowship with his wife and children? I am glad God was faithful to bring my family to me, after seventeen weeks and two days. Praise be to his name!

But the coming of my family presented its own set of difficulties. We started with the easier task—for our children to get education in high schools. People at Granada Heights Friends Church in La Mirada helped give counsel on how to go about it. With their help, we got all the children in school. The next problem was what Salome could do. Salome came to the States with a degree in community development and with rich experience in women ministries from her work with women in Kenya, Rwanda, and Congo. She was always busy in Africa, traveling to different countries and empowering women, mainly widows and single mothers who all called her "Mama Salome." On her arrival in the States, she was granted an F2 visa—one that is given to dependents of a student in the US. This visa does not allow the bearer to do anything, not even at the school of the student the bearer depends on. So, here was an African woman on an F2 visa, called to stay at home only, without any permission to do anything that can generate income on American soil!

Salome endured deep depression. She got sick in a way we could not understand. We went to many medical doctors, but they could not find the cause for her sickness. She would complain of headaches, sore muscles, abdominal pain, and many other symptoms that were difficult to understand. I am sure those who understand how culture shock operates can identify with Salome. Culture shock can take many forms; as Judith Lingenfelter defines the term, culture shock is "an emotional state of stress, depression, and varying degrees of impaired functions caused by constant exposure to people whose way of life conflicts with our own."[8]

Salome's recovery began when her Great Physician touched the area that was aching. The Great Physician, knowing what Salome was suffering from, opened the door for her to be with others in school—and that was enough for her healing. God, who understands that human beings are to work and not be idle day after day, touched the leadership at Biola University. Salome received a scholarship for her MA program in intercultural studies. Praise to Jesus, the Great Physician!

A LETTER FROM JESUS

As we were both studying at Biola University, we received tuition scholarships, but because of California law we had to raise funds for our medical insurance. Of course we also had to buy our own books. This is a lot of money for a family with children in school, and the situation was hard. Even today I actually cannot understand how we were able to pay for it all.

God worked through many individuals, but one day Jesus visited us through someone we did not know. Here is the story.

Salome and I were without money in our pocket—literally, we had nothing to eat. We would look at each other

8. Lingenfelter and Lingenfelter, *Teaching Cross-Culturally*, 121.

and almost cry. We decided to fast and pray. When we were praying in our room, we heard someone knocking at the door. I went to open the door and saw someone going away. The person seemed to be in his late twenties, with a beard and moustache. He had left a letter at our door. I thought it was a neighbor bringing me mail that had been mistakenly put in his mailbox. I took the letter and entered the house.

The envelope did not have a stamp. I opened it, and unfolded the paper inside. The letter said:

> I know you, my servants; I will always care for you.
> Do not worry about what you will eat or drink;
> I have chosen you,
> I will provide for you. For I am the Good Shepherd.

When I looked in the envelope there were ten bills of US $100, meaning $1,000. I began to tremble. I called Salome, and she came. She read the letter and asked me who had brought it. I told her about the young man I had seen. Salome concluded that this was fake money, and that we needed to check its authenticity. I asked her to accompany me to the Bank of America in La Mirada. We said to ourselves, "If the machine accepts it as we deposit it, then it will be authentic money." To our surprise, the machine accepted the money. We concluded that it was Jesus who had visited us that morning.

Salome and I know that the money came from someone. But how do you explain that coincidence of someone thinking about helping our family during the exact time of great need? Was this not God who spoke to that person and gave clear instructions to him to accomplish his purpose of providing for our needs? Before then, friends had put some cash money or gift cards in our mailbox at the university to help, but no one had given us more than $50. And here was someone sending $1,000!

Deep in our heart we believe it was Jesus who visited us that morning. We decided that we would keep that letter from generation to generation so that our children and grandchildren may know that our Lord is faithful, and that wonders and miracles continue to be done even today.

We have many other stories of our culture shock, but we need to move to the next question: How did we live with the "different other" in the USA? How did the different other impact us both positively and negatively? That is what the following section of this chapter deals with. I hope you are ready for more stories.

RACIAL EXPERIENCES

This book contains my personal experience, my journey with the different other. My ethics do not allow me to speculate, but only to say the truth about what I experienced. One question might be, "Is there racial discrimination in churches and Christian universities?" People shy away from discussing these issues, but these are everyday realities that we should face as human beings.

If I have to wrestle with the problem of communication and adjustment with Salome, my wife with whom I have lived for twenty-six years, how much more difficult would it be to live with a person from a different race and worldview? It may be baptized another name like tribalism or ethnocentricity, but it is the same sin. If you do not agree with me that there is racism in the USA, tell me why there are laws against "racial discrimination" in so many places? Why do we have interracial, multicultural, and diversity education in universities? Could lack of diversity in leadership in churches and totally homogeneous congregations or Christian organizations not communicate, sometimes, the seed of racism?

As we will discuss more in the next chapter, this is why we need *ubuntu*—to see the different other not as of the self's exclusion but as the self's continuation.

Let me say a few things about racism in general. First, racism does not necessarily mean discrimination of the minority. Any discrimination done on the basis of color is racism. White people can be racist as well as blacks and Asians.

Secondly, as we speak about racism, we do not mean that people should not have their distinctive culture. God wants me to be who I am as I follow him and to learn to do so more as I interact with those who are different from me.

Thirdly, we need to differentiate between classism and racism. There are classes among whites as there are among black and Asian people. So, if a white person becomes socially disadvantaged, it does not mean he is necessarily segregated against. The same applies to the black classes. A poor white person may access places of influence that even a rich black person may not access, if the community is of white racists, and a poor black person may also access a place of influence where a poor white person may not if the community is of black racists. So, we are speaking about racism here and not classism.

Thirdly, I would like to point out that in Rwanda, Burundi, Congo, the USA and everywhere, we have many myths that encourage and perpetuate racism. Such myths are at the root of statements like, "Luo people in Kenya are good administrators; Kikuyus are only good at business" or "Black people in the USA are lazy; whites are hardworking people" or "Tutsis are better leaders than Hutus." What a shame! All these are myths that need to be changed. We must stop our assumptions. We need to have a new perspective based on our identity in Christ who has created us all equal before him and complementary to each other. All of us are useful. That is what *Ubuntu*, understood biblically, is all about!

So far you may be saying, "Faustin, you are beating about the bush; tell us if you experienced racism while you were in the USA." First, I can confirm that there is racism in the USA because real sources told me that there is racism. For instance, one of my close friends from church told me how his father was racist. This friend of mine is a born-again Christian who loves my family very much. I have never seen any form of racism in him or his family, but he confirmed to me that his father was racist. Secondly, I have seen videos and heard testimonies from Biola students—whites, blacks and Asians—about racism within their work, their dormitories, and other places. Thirdly, racism is there in churches and universities because I have attended several conferences and workshops dealing with how to avoid racism. I have also listened to several messages in churches calling people to stop favoritism and racial segregation. I can therefore deduce that racism is a reality in churches and Christian universities in the USA.

But have I personally been victim of racism? The answer is no. Rather, people from other races have been very helpful to me and my family.

Primarily, I have learned that people of other colors are as fallen as I am. We are all sons and daughters of the first Adam. As such, we have all come short of the glory of God and need grace from the Second Adam. That discovery has removed some of the wrong presuppositions that I had as an African. White people, Asians, Latin Americans—they are all fallen people like Africans, struggling with the same problems of "self," which wants its own gratification. Today, if a white person does something wrong to me, I would conclude that he does it to me because of his heart, not because of his color. If you do not agree with me, tell me, have there not been black people devouring each other for their selfish ambition? Have you not seen the same among white people?

Another important attitude I have learned is to always seek to understand the different other so that I may avoid presumptions. Many problems between people of different colors are due to miscommunication; they are not really color issues. Miscommunication is something I have always feared during my time with the different other in the USA. This communication breakdown could be verbal or nonverbal.

And though Americans share culture, they have many subcultures too. African Americans, for example, have some subcultures that they developed as a result of the slavery that lasted many years. As they relate to white people, there could be clash of culture that may be interpreted as racism.

Please understand that I am not saying there is not racism! This is actually the reason why I have had several cultural informants whom I would always consult so that I may not make terrible mistakes.

TRANSFORMED BY LOVE FROM MY STUDENTS OF VARIOUS COLORS

During the five years that I worked on my doctorate at Biola University, I had the privilege to serve as an adjunct professor for four years, teaching a graduate class on African theology and undergraduate classes on both postcolonial African history and the French language. I was transformed by seeing how students would connect and help each other, especially in my language classes. Two specific cases are when I had black students in my class. For two years of my teaching I only had white students and a few Asians, and I would wonder why black students would not register for my class.

During my third year of teaching came a girl, Ayodele, the only black student among eighteen students. She was sharp and spoke French as someone born in Paris. I do not exaggerate; her accent was without linguistic interference. But above all these qualities, Ayodele was a humble lady with a great interpersonal gift. Most of the time, her colleagues would surround her asking her questions, and they would always laugh together and study together. When I would send someone to do an exercise on the blackboard who was not very confident, he or she would look back and whisper "Ayodele!" to make sure she affirmed the answer.

The other case is that of Brittany. Brittany was also brilliant and had an exceptional interpersonal gift. My French classes usually began at 8:30 a.m., and most mornings I arrived early, as any teacher would do. What was transformative for me was encountering Brittany with a group of her colleagues on the floor—literally on the floor—crying before the Lord and ministering to one another.

This scene was familiar to me from Africa, where we always saw people lying down on what we call "holy ground" and calling upon the Holy Spirit to come and take control. But for all the years I had been in the States, I had not seen such a practice. I remember several times Brittany and her friends would cry with tears flowing, and at the end I would hear them laughing and ministering to one another, holding hands with one another. It was fabulous for me; it was transformative.

These two cases, and many others I encountered, convince me that there is hope in our young generation because, it seems to me, these young people do not care about color, unless we in our family teach them wrong things. The stereotypes that some of us have will disappear as time passes. For example, in the past some Europeans thought black people had inferior intellectual ability than white people. What a mistake! Black people only lacked opportunities.

I am passionate about going back to Africa to give African students the same knowledge I gave to American students, so that my people may be equipped to enter into a rendezvous of giving and receiving with Americans, Europeans, Asians, and others. I trust the intellectual ability of my people and I know that, given an opportunity, Africans will do very well. We need Ayodeles and Brittanys in America as well as in Africa. Above all, we need our children to interact with each other just as Ayodele and Brittany interacted with their colleagues, with equal capacity and mutual respect. This is one of the ways that studying, living, and teaching at Biola has transformed me—I have been able to see firsthand the kind of interaction students can have together to bring hope and care to each other.

MORE TRANSFORMATION FROM MY STUDENTS

I have many stories about the good times I spent with my students. I loved them and they loved me too. Teaching and mentoring young people gives me great joy. My students have told me that one transformative aspect of our time together was my openness with them. I was not shy to share my life and struggles with my students. We always began class with prayer, and I taught every student to pray in French. But when it came to serious situations, such as a student who had lost a close relative, we would pray in English so that everyone would be in agreement with what we would be asking the Lord.

This was important because communication involves cognitive as well as affective dimensions. Praying for someone going through pain requires praying cognitively as well as affectively. That is why using a language that flows is important during such a time. Here is a story that relates such a dynamic.

One day I came to class when I was utterly exhausted. I was working on my dissertation and several other speaking engagements, and my son Pierre was going through a difficult time finding a school to transfer to from Cerritos College. I was exhausted spiritually, emotionally, and physically. I decided to share this with my class. Then I asked, "Could someone led by the Spirit please pray for me?" Everyone closed their eyes, and I heard Tabitha pray. Tabitha's prayer was prophetic and was full of the power of the Holy Spirit so that when she prayed I felt healing taking place in my body. I did not want to comment right after she prayed because it would have been too soon to conclude about the healing, but the whole day I was renewed. I had another French class at night, and I shared with the class what had happened that morning. We praised God together for touching my life through the prayer of one of my students. God is ready to minister to us through our students and any other person; we just need the humility to share what we are going through.

TRANSFORMED BY COLLEAGUES FROM OTHER WORLDVIEWS

When I came to the States, I knew the Lord was calling me to be better equipped for my people. I knew God's vision, but I needed a strategy to achieve it. So after six months, I gathered my closest friends and we registered TLAfrica. I arrived in California in August 2007, and in April 2008 TLAfrica received its official registration.

To confirm his vision to me, God opened the door for my wife and me to travel back to Africa that first summer. We went back to train our pastors with our friend, Pastor Paul Cannings of Living Word Fellowship Church in Houston, Texas. Since then, we have been going back to Africa every summer to train leaders and empower them for holistic transformation. Furthermore, the vision for a university (which I will address in the final part of this book) is not a new vision, but a continuation of our passion to see our people transformed and empowered to transform their communities. God has brought a great leadership team to Salome and me, and we have been transformed by working with such a diverse group. Can you imagine?—we have had on our US board an African American, a black from the Bahamas, a Korean American, a Chinese American, a black African (me) and several Caucasians. What a blessing in the diversity of the Body of Christ!

At the 2009 Leadership Training in Ruhengeri, Rwanda, Pastor Cannings came with two other pastors and three women from his church (all African Americans); we also had Pastor Shawn from Crossbridge Community Church in San Antonio (who was white), and Salome and me. What a picture of *ubuntu*, of unity with the different other! I particularly remember when it came to answering questions in the evening after class. All the facilitators would stand at the stage, and pastors-in-training would ask their questions. Those questions that Pastor Cannings would not answer, Pastor Shawn would answer, or the other pastors from Houston would, or I would. Just stop a moment and hang that picture on the wall of your heart. We will never forget the blessings in that conference! Join me to thank God for the transformative blessings of diversity in the Body of Christ.

DIVERSITY AT THE PULPIT:
UNBELIEVABLE BUT TRUE

I am sure some will be shocked to hear this story. The reason they may be shocked is that the art of preaching called "homiletics" that I have learned in the Western curriculum allows only one person to stand at the pulpit as he or she preaches. I have seen pastors interviewing people as they preach, but I have not seen three people speaking at the pulpit at the same time. Yet, if done well, it can be a blessing to the Body of Christ. And that is what we did when Ivan Chung, Director of International Students at Biola University, and Dr. Doris Ngaujah, who graduated from the intercultural doctoral program at Biola University, both visited my church and ministry in the summer of 2009.

On a Sunday, we went to fellowship at my former church, Limuru Town Baptist Church, and prepared a sermon on forgiveness that required Doris to share the stories of slavery in the States and the need for African Americans to forgive. Ivan shared about the need for forgiveness among Korean and Chinese younger versus older generations, and I shared about forgiveness in Rwanda and Kenya. My church at Limuru, which is located in an area of Kikuyus, had done her best to protect Mr. Moses Omolo— a Luo brother in the Lord who directed the choir in the church—when the Kikuyu militia wanted to kill him. So, for Doris and Ivan and me to speak about forgiveness was relevant to people at Limuru Town Baptist Church.

Doris began. She spoke about the evil of slavery and the need for the generation of African Americans today to let it go, instead of being enslaved by the past, even as they take lessons from the past. As some of you know, most African Americans are good at communication, and so is Doris. After fifteen minutes she had to stop and pass the pulpit to Ivan, but people wanted to hear more of her stories. I remember what her interpreter Ndungu did. When Doris said "God bless you," Ndungu said, "But that was only *ki-onjo*," which means, "That was only an appetizer!"

When Ivan came to the pulpit, people did not know the context of Koreans and Chinese, so it was a good learning experience for them. They related with the challenges of generational gap because with globalization and modernity, Africa is also going through such a time, where the new generation (*dot-com*) thinks the *wazee* (old people) are so old-fashioned that they cannot provide direction. The old people see the *dot-com* generation as people without morals and who could therefore bring a curse on the land.

After Ivan spoke, I concluded the message by calling people to forgiveness and challenging them to take the message of forgiveness to their families and communities. I quoted Desmond Tutu and told them, "Without forgiveness there is no future for Kenya" to powerfully end the message. What a display of beauty in diversity!

COACHED BY MY STAFF

In the fall of 2009, I taught a course on postcolonial African history at Biola University. All six students in my class loved to hear about Africa. Specifically, two of my students became more interested with what was happening in Africa. One of them, Karen Myers, who graduated in 2010, has played a transformative role in our ministry. After she graduated, she went to France for one semester, and when she returned I asked her whether we could serve together. She accepted. She is a missionary now working with TLAfrica in communication. Salome and I have met Karen's family in Kansas, and we have enjoyed our relationship with Karen and her family.

One thing Karen has done for me is to clue me in on American culture, especially on how to communicate with an American audience. She edits all my messages on the website, but she also writes most of the sensitive letters to donors under my direction. She is actually the one who read the first draft of this book and helped me know the sensitive issues throughout it. My wife and I consider her to be our cultural informant in matters of cross-cultural communication.

One day, Salome and I had time of prayer with Karen, and she could not understand why we could continue to suffer from lack of means to help our children in school when we are serving the Lord. She asked me whether I had shared my needs with donors and board members. I told her, "Board members are my friends, so they all know I do not have money to pay for my children." Karen asked me, "Have you shared the specific need of these school fees with the board members?" I said, "Karen, they love me, and they pray for me. I am sure even without telling them, they know that I need funds to pay for my children in school." Karen helped me understand that in the American culture, you do not assume that your friends know your needs; you need to express them directly, especially if they are friends. Karen was able to help Salome and me to understand this fundraising cultural practice in the States, and we continue to grow in the understanding of the American culture. We are not yet there, but we are growing.

As an African leader, I am happy to travel to different places and speak about how pastors in Ruhengeri, Rwanda, and widows in Bungoma, Kenya, need cows. But it is hard for me to express my needs. I always assume that people who hear my stories and know that Salome and I are students should conclude that we need help. That is the

African culture. You let people see your needs, then they themselves take the initiative to assist.

Well, has that changed? Not really. I understand it in my head, but it is difficult to follow. My initial suggestion to my fellow brethren on the US board was to help me raise funds for my family while I dealt with the needs of ministry. But again, my friends on the board who love me dearly told me, "Faustin, we do not have your stories; we cannot raise funds for you!" But I have appreciated Karen for the courage to clue me in on the best practice for expressing one's needs.

A CO-LABORER FOR THE PULPIT

It is not easy to communicate cross-culturally. That is why I always seek help and information for many situations of my communication. Regarding important speaking engagements, I have always consulted my friend and mentor, Pastor Ed. He is a wise man who loves me and desires to see me grow in my personal walk with Christ and my ministry. I always work on my message and I send it to him for feedback. Specifically, Ed has helped me choose the best illustrations to use in my sermons. That has helped me improve my messages as I speak in American churches.

One of my hardest speaking engagements was when I was asked to speak at Crossbridge Community church in San Antonio, Texas, in November 2011. The problem was that the missions pastor had asked me to speak on "spending less." The church was educating her members to spend less at Thanksgiving and Christmas, so that they may help the orphans in Haiti, buy cows for pastors in Byumba, Rwanda, and help other needy people in the community around them. The problem for me was to figure out how I—a Rwandan with no means here in the USA, coming from a background of far less means than people in the States—could teach Americans how to spend less.

But when I talked with Ed, he rather thought I was qualified to teach Americans how to spend less, and he helped me find a powerful way to teach the congregation. Ed said, "Faustin, just give your testimony on how in your life you have been content with little, then let the Scripture speak for itself." So, after I read 1 Timothy 6:17–19, here is how I introduced my sermon:

> Spending less! Uhh! As you know I am not from your culture, so I cannot directly teach you how to spend less. But I can share my story of God's faithfulness, which is far more powerful than possessions. I have the experience of contentment with using less and I have also helped others using the little I had. I have made sacrifices for the sake of others—for the sake of God's kingdom.

This introduction was a good entry into the sermon. After I shared my stories, I did some exposition of 1 Timothy 6, drawing some lessons from the passage. Those listening received the message well, and I thanked God for being able to communicate this difficult message to an audience of a different worldview.

Ed and I have been friends since I joined Granada Heights Friends Church in 2007, and for his two trips to Africa to train pastors in 2009 and 2010 we worked together to make sure his teachings were contextual. Ed teaches about biblical marriage, and as you read in chapter 1, his teaching has truly impacted my people in Africa. But before he taught, I needed to read his illustrations to make sure they were relevant to his listeners. No wonder when he teaches, the teaching pierces the heart of the receiver, just as Peter's sermon on the day of Pentecost.

In chapter 1 I shared how powerful Ed's teaching was in Rwanda. Even at Granada in the States, Ed's teaching is always transformative. My family has been blessed by his teachings so much that I will miss them when I return to Africa. But there is good news; with technology I can hear his sermons online!

MENTORED BY A TRIO OF ACADEMICS

My doctoral dissertation was supervised by a Korean American scholar. He is a graduate of Trinity International University and was mentored by the famous educator Dr. Ted Ward. My second reader was the director of the PhD and EdD programs at Talbot School of Theology, Biola University. This is the man who mainly shaped me because I took most of my doctoral classes with him. Furthermore, I was one of the doctoral students in his accountability group. For my third reader, I had the privilege of working with a man whom we Africans call *mzee wa kazi*, a Swahili expression meaning the most experienced elder. Indeed, this theology professor who sat on my doctoral committee is *mzee* wa *kazi*, and it was transformative for me to work with him during my dissertation journey.

What I noticed during the two years of writing my dissertation was that the trio had different approaches, all that I liked. The doctoral programs' director and the theology professor had some similarity that they both read my work and gave me written feedback. But the theology professor was so detailed that he would give me no less than two pages of mistakes, including grammatical and typing errors in the dissertation draft. The director of the doctoral programs would also make some corrections, but would rather be concerned about methodology, format, and the big picture of the dissertation. He would give me the hard copy of the draft while the theology professor would sit with me and go through the document page by page.

My main advisor was different from his two colleagues. During our appointments, we would discuss the general ideas of my dissertation, leaving me to work out the details. He would use the Socratic method to draw out my thoughts, so that in the end I would write what I truly believed. He would say, "Faustin, always remember that this is *your* work."

What was common in the three advisors was that they were all encouragers. But each one also brought something unique that I needed. My main advisor took me as a doctoral candidate and trusted that once we discussed an idea, I would be able to direct myself. He always called me a self-motivated student. My doctoral director was thorough in checking on the format of the dissertation and giving feedback on the methodology chapter. I also appreciated the theology professor's way of correcting even grammatical errors because by the end of each chapter there was no more need for editing further. In fact, in the third chapter that the theology professor advised me on entirely, the person doing the final edit did not find any errors at all!

This is another example of the beauty of diversity, with a black student working with an Asian American main advisor and two Caucasians on the dissertation committee. I loved my work. The entire process and the whole journey and product were transformative for me. I enjoyed my relationship with the three advisors, and I was happy with my findings and the final product of my dissertation.

SUMMARY

Differences in color, tribe, and worldview can constitute exclusion from one's being or contribute an extension of one's being. When we visit different places and meet and interact with different people, we can discover many new ways to see the world. That is transformation. We, however, need to be ready to learn and humble ourselves in order to learn from these experiences and persons who might have experiences to share with us. God can use anything—a stoplight or a cell phone—or any person—a student or a dissertation advisor—to mold our lives into his image.

Furthermore, this transformation that affects both host and visitor is happening for us in an unprecedented way. As Manuel Ortiz and Susan Baker explain, with globalization, "The mission field has skipped across the ocean into our neighborhoods and local church communities."[9] What an opportunity for a rendezvous of giving and receiving. Is this not God's desire for the members of his Body to be diverse, complementary, and interdependent, as it says in 1 Corinthians 12? Churches that fail to understand this mutual relationship will fall short of God's blessings coming through globalization. The same applies to universities. Research has shown that higher education's achievement in preparing students for success in an increasingly diverse society and global marketplace will depend on how successful institutions are considering diversity.[10] Learning in a diverse environment brings new perspectives to the way the learner sees the world.

Again, let's acknowledge that encountering the different other is not easy. That is why understanding *ubuntu* is a necessity not just for Africans but for all humankind. We all need *ubuntu*—but what is *ubuntu*, and why do we really need it? Let's move on to chapter 3.

---

9. Ortiz and Baker, *Urban Face of Mission*, 49.

10. Abadeer, "Seeking Redemptive Diversity"; Jayakumar, "Can Higher Education?"

3

Ubuntu as a Remedy

I AM AWARE THAT some readers may be wondering what *ubuntu* is all about. Don't worry; I will fly high so that we may avoid turbulence. I will do my best to navigate difficult terms so that our communication may create understanding.

Let me try to explain what *ubuntu* is in simple terms. Let's compare a person to a brass string. A guitar has several brass strings. One isolated brass string may not produce music, unless it is played with several others. However, the one string has a place on the guitar, just as all the brass strings do. An African proverb says, "One brass wire cannot produce a sound." *Ubuntu* seeks to value a person and the community in which the person lives. We will come to it on a deeper level later in this chapter, but for now let's talk about its recent development.

Although the *ubuntu* philosophy is as old as the earth, we owe its recent development to Archbishop Desmond Tutu, a man who experienced firsthand the apartheid system in South Africa, where he was born, grew up, and ministered. He was an eyewitness to both the inauguration of apartheid in 1948 and its legal removal in 1990. When Nelson Mandela was released in 1990 after twenty-seven years of imprisonment, he spent his first night of freedom in Bishop Tutu's court. After President Nelson Mandela took power, the South African parliament established the Truth and Reconciliation Commission (TRC), headed by Bishop Tutu, which completed its task in June 1998. According to Wilhelm Verwoerd,[1] the TRC tasks were:

a) "to get as complete a picture of the nature, causes and extent of politically motivated gross human rights violations which occurred between March 1, 1960, and May 10, 1994;

b) to help restore the human and civil dignity of victims by granting them an opportunity to relate their own accounts of the violations;

c) to grant amnesty to those individuals giving "full disclosure" of politically motivated crimes during this period; and

d) to make recommendations to the President and Parliament on reparation and rehabilitation measures to be taken, including measures preventing the future commission of human rights violations."

Verwoerd[2] explains four roles of the TRC in restorative justice. First, the process seeks to redefine crime. It shifts the primary focus of crime from the breaking of laws or offenses against a faceless state to a perception of crime as violations against human beings, as injury or wrong to another person. Second, it is based on reparation. It aims at the healing and the restoration of all concerned—victims, offenders, their families, and the larger community. Third,

---

1. Verwoerd, "Individual and/or Social Justice," 117.
2. Ibid., 124–25.

it encourages victims, offenders, and the community to be directly involved in resolving conflict with the state and legal professionals acting as facilitators. Finally, it supports a criminal justice system that aims at keeping offenders accountable through the full participation of both victims and offenders in righting the wrong.

When Desmond Tutu was appointed the chair of TRC, he already shared the philosophy of reconciliation with Nelson Mandela and Thabo Mbeki—respect for a person's dignity regardless of what that person had done. Condemning apartheid, Tutu warned, "The oppressed could become tomorrow's oppressors because sin is an ever-present possibility."[3] This is the rationale for *ubuntu*.

Ubuntu means "humanity" and is related to *umuntu*, which is the category of "intelligent human force."[4] Tutu defines *ubuntu* as the person who is welcoming, hospitable, warm and generous, affirming of others, and who does not feel threatened that others are able and good; this person has a proper self-assurance that comes from knowing he or she belongs to a greater whole and realizes that he or she is diminished when another is humiliated, tortured, oppressed, or threatened.[5]

In other African languages, such as Kiswahili and Kinyarwanda, *ubuntu* designates quality. So, Tutu's second definition brings an important addition to the first definition when it highlights this idea of quality. For example, in Kiswahili, a person is *mtu*, and the quality of a person is *utu*, which means humanity. A person who kills another is said to have lost his *utu*. *Ubuntu* is the quality of *umuntu*, which means that a person's humanness achieves this deeper, more lasting level of quality when the *umuntu* does what

3. Qouted in Battle, *Reconciliation*, 3.
4. Ibid., 39.
5. Ibid., 35.

Tutu describes in his first definition: being warm and generous, knowing that oneself is diminished when another is diminished. This deeper, resounding quality of humanness—though transforming the interior of a person—actually happens in an exterior setting: for *ubuntu* lives in the context of relationships.

Now, you may have already noticed that relationship is key to the African worldview. While Descartes' edict, "I think, therefore I am," represents the Western worldview, the African society would rather argue, "I belong by blood relationship, therefore I am." There is meaning and purpose to his life only because he belongs to a family, a clan, and a tribe. Tutu then translates *ubuntu* from the context of family to one of community, which is proper because, as Dianne Stinton writes, "A cardinal point in African anthropology is that individual identity is established and fulfilled only in context of community."[6]

Also, by stating that a person "is diminished when others are diminished," Tutu implicitly brings the notion of interdependence. In Africa, for example, a force can increase or decrease through interaction with another. For instance, when I gain a new friend, my force increases as well as my friend's force. From the same perspective, if I have a problem with my friend and we are not able to reconcile, our forces decrease.

Using the language of Miroslav Volf,[7] "the exclusion of the other" does not increase force but rather diminishes it. This is why in the African tradition, even when someone treats others in the community poorly, the community disciplines the wrongdoer instead of excluding him or her from the community, for excluding him or her would decrease the force of both the wrongdoer and the entire community!

6. Stinton, *Jesus of Africa*, 145.
7. *Volf, Exclusion and Embrace.*

Likewise, unity between people increases their individual forces as well as the force of the whole community.

This has some logic. First, when people are in conflict, they cannot achieve much—even in the physical realm—because their energy is focused on the disagreement. Secondly, in the spiritual realm, the spiritual force of those who are in conflict decreases. Their prayer to *Imana* (God in Kinyarwanda) cannot be heard, for *Imana* cannot hear the prayer of a person with anger and bitterness. Thirdly, Satan takes advantage of their bitterness by taking away their joy. Consequently, their spiritual force decreases. Finally, when people are in conflict with each other, it is difficult to do something for the church and the community. Therefore, this decreases the force of the church and the community as well. In addition, if the conflict is not solved, *Imana* may be angry against the people in conflict and may punish them, and sometimes this punishment may affect the community.

Jean Hatzfield points out the danger of dehumanizing each other in the case of genocide in Rwanda. He says, "While these men (perpetrators) have committed appalling crimes, they are still men."[8] The dehumanization of victims involves categorizing a group as inhuman either by using categories of subhuman creatures (that is, animals) or by using categories of negatively evaluated unhuman creatures (such as demons or monsters). Those who committed the genocide dehumanized the victims even before they killed them, when they called them different names such as cockroaches. *Ubuntu* theology is needed here so that everyone is able to consider another as human. Indeed, the lack of *ubuntu* is devastating, for when someone considers another as subhuman, they are also partaking of that identity.

Aimé Césaire, in his *Discourse on Colonialism*, describes colonialism as a "relations of domination and

8. Hatzfield, *Time for Machetes*, 31.

submission which turn the colonizing man into a classroom monitor, an army sergeant, a prison guard, a slave
driver, and the indigenous man into an instrument of
production."[9] This is what Césaire calls "thingification"
(*chosification* in French), because both the colonized and
colonizer take on new identities. The idea of "thingification" was further developed by John Kasyoka, who cites
Buber[10] speaking about the relationship between "I" and
"It" and "I" and "You." Kasyoka[11] explains that the "I-It"
relationship is one of having, using, exploiting, and pos-
sessing. It is a one-way relationship, from subject to object,
from "I" to a thing. Kasyoka says that there is no mutual
understanding between these two parties. Buber points out
that we become human only through genuine human relationships, and we lose something of our own humanness in
the "I-It" relationship. He gives an example of a master and
slave and concludes that in this relationship both parties
are dehumanized. But another kind of relationship exists.
Buber explains how the "I-You" relationship involves our
whole being and calls for a response from the whole being
of the other.

Clearly, *ubuntu* helps the offender and the victim become truly human because they can see the different other
as human. On the one side, it is true that ontologically,
every human being is created with the capacity to do what
is good, because we are all created in God's image. Many
years before Christ, Greek philosophers such as Aristotle
recognized that every human being has a sense of law in the
heart. The same idea was reinforced by St. Thomas Aquinas,
who "was fundamentally concerned with law as the basis

9. Césaire, *Discourse on Colonialism*, 42.

10. Buber, *I and Thou*.

11. Kasyoka, *Introduction to Philosophy of Religion*, 18–19.

of social harmony."[12] This means that there is no excuse for even unbelievers not doing good, for, as the Apostle Paul puts it, "Although they know God's righteous decree that those who do such things deserve death, they not only continue to do these very things but also approve of those who practice them" (Rom 1:32).

On the other side, as the apostle Paul puts it, human beings have become rebellious in their will because "The human heart was darkened" because of sin (Rom 1:21). Before salvation, the human being is self-centered—thinking, deciding and acting as a little god. But from the moment one surrenders life to the true God, the Creator and Redeemer, Christ sends light into the darkened heart so that the human being may be able to see God in his glory and other human beings as created in the same image. This was possible through his death at the cross that removed the wrath of the just God. It is at the cross of Christ that the transformation of our thoughts, will, perceptions, and relationships take place in a lasting way. It is at the cross that the victim has more spiritual power to see the enemy as a human being worthy of respect and dignity, even if the offender does not deserve it. This is because salvation is a free gift that is given to an undeserving beneficiary who should therefore express the same grace to others.

Now that we have crossed the winding mountains of philosophy and theory, let's come back to some stories. Let's see how we all need *ubuntu*.

RWANDA NEEDS UBUNTU

The conflict among Rwandans that culminated in the 1994 genocide, killing 800,000 Tutsis and moderate Hutus,

12. Krapiec, *Person and Natural Law*, 32.

remains difficult to understand. How can we understand that people who lived together for many centuries—speaking the same language, sharing the same culture, intermarrying and giving each other cows as signs of close relationships—could turn and kill each other? Historians have written about the immediate and long-term causes of this genocide. But far from entering into social or political debates, my passion is rather to wrestle with the question, "How can the *ubuntu* philosophical worldview be a foundation for unity among Rwandans and a source for increasing force among people living in the same nation?"

My assumption is that unity among Rwandans—which should lead to an increase of force, a rich thriving, for all—is possible only if Rwandans learn from the relationship between the community of the Trinity and the increase of force in Christ by the paradox of the cross. I say "paradox" because in the African worldview, especially the Bantu worldview, the cross could be viewed as a decrease of force. Yet, examined from the biblical perspective, the cross extraordinarily increases the force that defeated the devil and his powers, breaking the fortress that separated God and man and Jews and Gentiles. From this conclusion, we hope that people in Rwanda will reconcile following the *ubuntu* principle, which finds its reality in the communal unity of the Trinity, which itself is totally embodied in the sacrificial love of the cross. The ethnic divisions will be transformed into a community of united Rwandans who will prosper spiritually and socially, and who will contribute to the development of their nation.

A SHORT BACKGROUND TO THE PROBLEM OF RWANDANS

Many people who read about what happened in Rwanda believe the issue in Rwanda is mainly an ethnic problem. Janine Clark[13] is of the opinion that the genocide resulted from preexisting, deeply-seated ethnic hatreds. Others think that the main problem among Rwandans is rather a problem of injustice and exclusion, which uses ethnic identity as a means of understanding the problem. In this case, the deep cause of the problem resides in man's evil heart of selfishness and pride. Charles Mironko's research supports this opinion: the perpetrators of the genocide pointed out, "we Rwandans lived like brothers and sisters" and "[Hutus and Tutsis] got on well."[14] In contrast, Hatzfield's interviews suggest that jealousy and old grievances—as opposed to ethnic hatred—motivated some people to kill.

Historically, the problem in Rwanda has been a problem of exclusion for many years. Volf's *Exclusion and Embrace* is a theological response to the suffering that people in the world, especially his people, have endured as a result of exclusion and injustice. He maintains that "exclusion" is both the exclusion of the other from one's heart and from one's world. For Volf, that is a sin, for "it is the kind of purity that wants the world cleansed of the other rather than the heart cleansed of the evil that drives people out by calling those who are clean 'unclean' and refusing to help make clean those who are unclean."[15]

This too is the problem that has ruled in Rwanda for many years, not just because of ethnic divisions—for even among Hutus there is exclusion based on regionalism

13. Clark, *Learning from the Past.*
14. Mironko, "Ibitero," 171.
15. Volf, *Exclusion and Embrace*, 74.

(Kiga/North versus Nduga/South), and among Tutsis there is exclusion based on clanism (Banyiginya versus Bega), as well as exclusion based on nationalism (those who grew up in Uganda versus those who grew up in other countries). Volf says the primary problem is sin that classifies people and puts them into categories. This is the wickedness of stereotypes.

Unfortunately, this categorization of stereotyping does not have a basis for people who share the same land, culture, and ancestry. Some may deny the fact that they share ancestry, yet every Rwandan agrees that *Imana* is the creator of all. For Christians who read the Bible, they all agree that we all come from Adam, and from Noah after the flood. In addition, the history of Africa explains that immigrants from other places inhabit most countries today. For instance, Shaba, the former Katanga in Congo, is inhabited by people who migrated from Zambia. The Nande and Hunde living in Eastern Congo migrated from Uganda. Many Bakongo living in Bas-Congo in the Democratic Republic of Congo migrated from Angola. So, insisting that Tutsis came from Ethiopia to inhabit Rwanda should not be a reason for both groups to develop hatred against each other. This explanation reveals that exclusion and injustice in Rwanda have no rationale other than selfishness and pride.

Furthermore, the Western mindset of favoring and categorizing some as superior and more capable of ruling only aggravated the problem in Rwanda. The Belgians, like the Germans before them, saw the Tutsis as the superior race, and this prejudice became deeply rooted in their administrative structures and policies. Paul Timothy Longman[16] also explains that in the 1950s, the Catholic Church abandoned its support for the Tutsi minority hegemony and threw its weight behind the Hutu majority. Unfortu-

16. Longman, *Christianity and Genocide in Rwanda.*

nately, in independent Rwanda this merely reversed the stereotypes and left the Tutsi as a vulnerable and discriminated minority.

It is clear that Westerners have had some involvement in what happened in Rwanda, but did they push Rwandans to kill each other? No! Rwandans, therefore, should be the first to bear the responsibility for what happened in Rwanda. In addition, Rwandans should seek a way to regain and restore humanness in their hearts. Rwandans need the *ubuntu* sense in their hearts for the healing of their nation.

EUROPE NEEDS UBUNTU

The genocide did not happen in Rwanda because people were illiterate or were not from an advanced society in matters of education and technology; it happened because of man's heart. JanineClark 2009, who conducted research on the Rwandan genocide concludes, "Genocide can happen anywhere under certain conditions. No country is immune."[17] No country is immune, for it happened in Europe before it happened in Africa. Billy Graham and his wife, Ruth, traveled to Europe some years ago and visited the Nazi death camp of Auschwitz in Poland. After laying a memorial wreath and kneeling to pray at a wall in the middle of the camp where twenty thousand people had been shot, Graham became almost speechless. He asked himself, "How could such a terrible thing happen—planned and carried out by a nation that had produced some of the most highly educated people in the world?"[18] Graham concluded,

17. Clark. "Learning from the Past," 18.
18. Graham, *Key to Personal Peace*, 12.

"Our soul has a disease that is worse than any dreaded cancer or heart disease we can face."[19]

Did you know that the current racial problem that Europe is experiencing is a consequence of some of the solutions that European countries suggested during their economic growth? In the 1950s and 1960s Western Europe—especially the "Golden Triangle" of Birmingham, Milan, and Dusseldorf—was undergoing economic expansion. It needed more labor than it could recruit from its own rural areas. As W. J. Milligan explains, the solution was that the "Turks and West Natives, North Africans and Asians came to the cities of Europe in response to the invitations of government and commerce to provide a new work force, and to do some of the dirty jobs which the indigenous Europeans preferred not to do."[20] Unfortunately, Hohenberg continues, "When the economic tide turned and jobs became scarce, the new work force became surplus labor. The Europeans therefore began to say, 'Now "they" have become a part of "us."'" Since then, resentment of the outsiders has been widespread, notably in working-class districts where contacts at work and in school are close; and there is competition for housing and jobs."[21] This is a specific illustration of man's heart with its corrupt, selfish, and exploitative mind.

Generally, every problem that has a sociopolitical or economic face always has a deeper source in man's heart.

19. Ibid.

20. Milligan, *New Nomads*, 84, quoted in Conn and Ortiz, *Urban Ministry*, 71.

21. Hohenberg and Lees, *Making of Urban Europe*, 350, quoted in Conn and Ortiz, *Urban Ministry*, 71.

THE UNITED STATES NEEDS UBUNTU

Before I came to the States, I had learned about African Americans and the history of slavery, but I knew very little about Native Americans. My interest in the history of Natives Americans came recently after January of 2012, when I taught a course on African theology. During the course, one of my students, who was married to a Native American, often identified with what happened to black Africans during slavery and colonialism. This is when I began reading about Native American history. But my interest increased when, a month after I taught the course, I was invited to speak about forgiveness at Calvary Church in Souderton, Pennsylvania. One of my friends approached me and shared a situation that touched my heart. He said that he had visited and ministered at a school for Native American children. Suddenly one child came and told him, "You are bad; you have oppressed our people." My friend was in great pain, not because of what this child had said, but because of the education that Native American children might be receiving in their families. I did not answer my friend, but I empathized with him.

History traces the beginning of the problem between Europeans and Native Americans to Christopher Columbus, the explorer who expressed in a letter to Queen Isabella that he believed Native Americans "should be good servants."[22] This was of course "an assumption that Natives were inferior to Europeans," as Wright claims, an assumption that is contrary to *ubuntu*. Peter Martyr, an Italian humanist resident in the Spanish court, published in 1530 his *Decades of the New World* in which he characterized Native Americans as "creatures bearing resemblance to humans in form, but lacking the social, moral and intellectual quali-

22. Hurtado and Iverson, *Major Problems*, 46.

ties of civilized beings; gentle folk who lived simply and innocently, without enforcement of laws . . ."[23] It is not my intention to go into details here, but there were many long battles over four hundred years between Native Americans and the Europeans who had settled in the new land. Wright explains that during the battles between the Natives and the colonists, "colonists cut off the hands and heads of Natives they had killed and set them up on poles as warnings to others. Native Americans retaliated by burning towns and farms and carrying women and children off in captivity"[24] You can understand how some Native American people are angry with white Americans. But also, white Americans should not be victimized because of the evils that their ancestors did to the Native Americans. However, it is vitally important for white Americans to listen to the pain of Native Americans today. This is one reason why Americans need *ubuntu*.

In addition to the need for *ubuntu* between white Americans and Native Americans, there is also need for *ubuntu* between African Americans and white Americans. As a black African, one of my difficult classes as a French professor at Biola University was to read a text about how slaves were gathered and taken to an island in Senegal for an unknown destination.

I always shared with my students that history is there to teach us, but not to make us guilty. Most of the time, it was easy when I had only white students in my class. In two classes, I had a few African American students, and I would approach this class very carefully, not to offend the African Americans and not to make the white Americans feel guilty when they did not deserve to. The issue of slavery, just as the issue of displacing the Native Americans, was done

23. Stone, *Historiography of Genocide*, 277.

24. Ibid, 19.

for selfish interests. Read what Senator Henry Berry said in 1832 to the Virginia House of delegates concerning the state of slaves:

> We have, as far as possible, closed every avenue by which light may enter the slave's mind. If we could extinguish the capacity to see the light, our work would be complete. They would then be on the level with the beast of the field and we should be safe.[25]

Should African Americans hate the current generation of white Americans for this? No! Should African Americans be sad for this? Yes! Should white Americans be guilty of this? No! Should this teach white Americans something? Yes! That is why there is need for white Americans, Native Americans, and African Americans to meet at the cross of Jesus where they can see each other as created in God's image but corrupted by sin and redeemed by the shed blood of Christ, the Head of the Body of which Christians from each race and tribe are members, and in which there is no distinction of white, black, or any color, but all are children of God. There are so many more stories concerning so many more ethnicities in America. So many people have difficult stories and experiences to share here. All Americans need *ubuntu*!

UBUNTU PUT INTO PRACTICE

Our purpose in this section is to focus on the root cause of the problem of exclusion, which is nothing other than sin in the human heart. To borrow from Moltmann's ideas, how can the oppressed in Africa, Europe, and the USA be

25. Otabil, "Beyond the Rivers of Ethiopia, " 3, quoted in Adeyemo, *Is Africa Cursed?*, 15.

liberated from the suffering caused by oppression, and how can the oppressors be liberated from the injustice caused through oppression? Or, how can solidarity with the victims be formed and at the same time the perpetrators' transgressions be atoned for?[26] The goal of liberating both the oppressor and the victim should be, in the *ubuntu* perspective, to increase individuals' forces, and the whole force of their community. Instead of exclusion, we can forge relationships of inclusion that make people interrelated, interdependent, equal, and free.

This liberty and solidarity cannot be achieved unless the perpetrators and the oppressed meet at the cross, where Christ identified with the oppressed and atoned for the transgression of the oppressor, making them one—as he, his Father and the Holy Spirit are one. Christ's example calls on the new reconciled people to form a new community characterized by the unity found among the persons of the Trinity, which is the best way to illustrate unity in community. A biblical reflection on *ubuntu* serves both to prevent violence and to facilitate the reconciliation process. Because all people are created in God's image, *ubuntu* theology values both individuals and their relationships.

The Bible supports *ubuntu* theology. An example of this is 1 Corinthians 12:12–31, in which Paul wrote about unity in diversity. First, Paul explained that the Body of Christ is a new community of diverse people united by the Holy Spirit (vv. 12–13). Paul stated that this community can heal insecurities caused by diversity (vv. 14–18). This healing comes from recognizing that every part of the Body matters, because God has desired and arranged its ordering. Therefore, there is no reason for comparison between members, and no reason for feeling inferior. The Body

26. Moltmann, *Spirit of Life*, discussed in Volf, *Exclusion and Embrace*, 23.

exists to heal the ethnocentrism caused by pride, and in this new community no one may say, "I am self-sufficient; I do not need others; my race is superior to others" (vv. 19–24). Ironically, Paul stated that the seemingly weaker parts of the body are indispensable, and that the less honorable parts receive special honor (vv. 22–23). God also uses the new community to heal broken emotions (vv. 25–26).

Unity binds the members of the body together in love, enabling members to care for one another. This union, which takes place when people trust, accept, and care for each other, creates space for emotional healing. In such an environment, members of the body can use their gifts to serve others and not for selfish ambition. The thirteenth chapter of 1 Corinthians is a direct continuation of the twelfth chapter: those who exercise their spiritual gifts should do so because of love (vv.1–3). Paul encouraged a desire for gifts that equips *others*, such as apostleship, prophecy, or teaching, above gifts of power, such as signs, miracles, wonders, or utterance.

In 1 Corinthians we see four characteristics of *ubuntu* in the biblical context: unity in diversity through the power of the Holy Spirit; acknowledgement that one's position in the body of Christ depends on God's sovereign will; interdependence rather than self-sufficiency; and, as a mark of love, the desire to put others first. Brian Edgar,[27] who has written about this passage, indicates three themes that, according to me, could be lessons from *ubuntu* theology:

1. No one should think of their spiritual gift as a private possession. Edgar quotes David Prior, "Any tendency nowadays to talk of 'my church . . . my gifts . . . my ministry' can have Corinthian overtones."[28] In this

---

27. Edgar, *Message of the Trinity*, 267.

28. Prior, "Message of 1 Corinthians," 267, quoted in ibid.

first lesson, individuals think of their gifts not as primarily personal, but as tools to help others experience God's love.

2. In seeking gifts, the focus should be upon the whole body rather than the individual. Edgar advises believers to prioritize the health of the body before their own function of power. Is this not a contrast between "I think, therefore I am" and "I belong, therefore I am"?

3. The corporate nature of the gifts does not mean that they cannot be of great benefit to individuals, for as individuals are strengthened so too is the body.[29] Just as the Bible values both the church and its members, *ubuntu* theology honors both the community and the individual. Indeed, the great beauty of *ubuntu*, and Paul's vision of the church as body, is that the quality of the individual is truly important.

When I took biblical anthropology—as an undergraduate and graduate student—my professors asked the students to describe their expectations for the course. We expressed the desire to understand humanity in relation to itself, to God, and to others. By the end of these courses, we had covered issues regarding a person's constituents (soul, spirit, heart), and people in relation to God (humanity in God's image), but we never covered anything about people in relation to others. The issues we covered in defining the *imago Dei* were about cognition, affection, and volition, but we did not explore how these operate—and operate more *fully*—in the relational life of a person.

The explanation of such lack is simple: our professors were trained by mentors who viewed humanity through the lens of platonic philosophy. We need a biblical anthropology that also wrestles with the question of who people are in

29. Edgar, *Message of the Trinity*, 268.

relation to God and in relation to fellow human beings, an anthropology that explores how we come to know God and be known by him all the more fully when we are interacting with others in authentic, vulnerable, transformative ways. Such an anthropology could integrate knowledge of humanity and its existence in relation to God and community.

Dietrich Bonhoeffer wrote, "To disjoint theology from practice and focus on one aspect over the other is not theology at all!"[30] Individualistic theology has emphasized philosophical reflection more than Christian formation, for the latter primarily takes place in the context of relationships. When Jesus began his ministry, his first call to his disciples was not, "Memorize what I say" but "Follow me." Being with him, having his friendship, was more important than anything else. Therefore, if we agree that the task of theology is, as Ellen T. Charry explains, "To assist people to come to God as it was prior to the seventeenth century and the influence of modernism, then any theological reflection on humanity should consider people in the context of their relationships."[31]

Ubuntu theology is different from individualistic theologies for three reasons:

1. Because it concerns both individuals and their communities, *ubuntu* sustains harmonious relationships.

2. *Ubuntu* theology promotes holistic ministry, which addresses the spiritual, social, and economic needs of people who are suffering from personal sin and social injustice. *Ubuntu* promotes holistic ministry because it creates community between the local church (including Christian institutions) and the neighborhood—a community bound by mutual commitment

---

30. Burtness, "Shaping the Future," 25.

31. Charry, *By the Renewing of Your Minds*, 5.

and understanding. Transformation will not take place unless the vision of the church becomes deeply involved with the thriving of the neighborhood.

3. *Ubuntu* values both parties involved in conflict. Rahim, Buntzman, and White have defined integrated conflict management as a system that "involves high concern for self as well as the other party involved in the conflict."[32] Integrated conflict management is concerned with collaboration between parties—through openness, the exchange of information, and an examination of differences—to reach a solution acceptable to both. *Ubuntu* theology is related to integrated conflict management because it counts victim and offender—both having been created in God's image—as valuable. Only a system that recognizes the dignity of both parties can lead to true healing and reconciliation.

This is how *ubuntu* theology enables the restoration of force, leading to the uniting, liberating power of forgiveness. But offering forgiveness to the offender does not mean that *ubuntu* theology condones evil. Instead of offering temporal solutions through external punishments, *ubuntu* allows for transformation in the lives of victims and offenders. When victim and offender are able to meet and share from their hearts, peace is restored to the entire community. But transformation will not take place unless a person sees the other as oneself, and oneself as made in God's image. In order to be transformative, *ubuntu* must therefore include both horizontal and vertical dimensions. It must reflect the community of the Trinity (the vertical dimension) in order to see the person across the room (the horizontal dimension).

32. Rahim, Buntzman, and White, "Empirical Study," 158.

TRINITARIAN COMMUNITY AS THE MODEL FOR UBUNTU

The horizontal dimension or social function of *ubuntu* is insufficient to bring lasting transformation in racial and tribal reconciliation for many reasons. In the first place, a corrupt person can only love imperfectly. Such a love cannot endure. Martin Luther claimed, "Free will after the fall has the power to do good only in passive capacity, but it can always do evil in an active capacity."[33] If love is to be perfect and enduring, it must come from God, who alone is perfect and eternal. Indeed, God is love (1 John 4:16).

Also, social love is often contractual. For example, an employer may love his employee because of the benefit he receives from their relationship, and verse versa. Based on the Trinity, love from God sees beyond benefit and gives sacrificially. God sent his son Jesus to redeem us because his sacrifice would create his bride, the church—not because he had something to receive from us. If we truly love those from whom we differ, we should not require contracts stipulating what they will give when we forgive them. We should forgive sacrificially. Love and forgiveness give us the power to pray for our enemies, and to claim them for the Lord. As a result, they may come to know God's love and join us as members of Christ's Body.

A purely social perspective of *ubuntu* is utilitarian. It is based on the question, "What shall I gain from this relationship?"—even if that gain is simply social peace for the next decade. In contrast, a vertical perspective reminds us that Christ loved us when we were still sinners and that his love was an end in itself. While we were still sinners, Christ died for us, despite that he had nothing to gain from his relationship with us (Romans 5:8).

33. Wengert, *Pastoral Luther*, 52.

Additionally, a horizontal perspective of *ubuntu* is merely convenient. For instance, if you are working in an organization with someone you do not like, you may be talking to the person out of convenience—just because you are working together. But this does not mean that greeting the person reflects love. A vertical perspective of *ubuntu* enables us to truly love even when it is impossible to love. Jesus commanded his disciples to love even their enemies, or those who did not love the disciples.

It is only at the cross of Jesus that the victim can have power to meet and accept his offender; otherwise, humanly speaking, it is too hard. I shared previously the story of the woman who, in our trauma healing retreat in Kenya in 2003, shared for forty-five minutes about the killing of her nineteen relatives during the civil war in Bunia in the Democratic Republic of Congo. It is true she had difficulty saying, "I forgive them." But when she did so, she sighed as someone who puts down a heavy burden that was weighing on him or her. Friends, without the cross, *ubuntu* would be for the sake of convenience or utility or function or contract. But true love, which makes acceptance possible, is only found in the Trinity.

According to Scott Horrell, the Bible teaches about one God who eternally exists as three distinct centers of consciousness. Horrell has used the phrase "three distinct centers of consciousness" to mean "three persons," and he has defined person as "a center of self-consciousness *existing in relationship to others*."[34] Intrinsic to being alive is being in relationship; this is true not only for humans, but also for God. He does not exist outside of his relationship to the members of the Trinity. If the Creator himself is this

34. Horrell, "Eternal Son of God," 52. Emphasis added.

way, how much more is his creation? Referring to John 1, Horrell[35] explains that each divine person consists of:

1. the essential nature of Deity ("the Word was God")— that is, the attributes (*ousia* in Greek) that distinguish God from creation;

2. full self-consciousness ("I am"), the actual reality of self, distinct from other persons, which presupposes mental properties and internal relations;

3. unique relatedness ("the Word was with God"), distinguishing each member of the Godhead from the others in I-Thou relationships; and

4. *perichoresis* (I am in the Father and the Father in me"), the mutual indwelling of each in the other without confusion of self-consciousness. John 1:1 and 14 indicate that Jesus, the incarnate Word of God, is evidence of diversity within the Godhead. He is himself God, while at the same time being with God. The sentence, "In the beginning was the Word, and the Word was with God, and the Word was God" indicates that unity and diversity exist simultaneously in the Godhead (v. 1).

In the Gospel of John, Jesus says, "Do you not believe that I am in the Father, and the Father is in me? The words that I say to you I do not speak on my own initiative, but the Father abiding in me does his works" (14:10). Jesus teaches the disciples that they cannot bear fruit on their own; *perichoresis* must also exist between him and his followers (John 15:1–5). The fruit the disciples are to bear is love for one another, and in this the disciples also demonstrate their love for Christ. By loving God and man, the disciples fulfill the two greatest commandments (Mark 12:28–31).

35. Ibid.

In John 17:20, Jesus takes perichoretic or "indwelling" language and applies it to the entire church. Jesus prays for the church to be one as he and the Father are one (17:11, 21, 22–23). He defines this relationally indwelling unity in perichoretic terms, praying "that they may all be one; even as you, Father, are in me and I in you" (17:21). Jesus continues, repeating his beautiful petition: "That they may be one, just as we are one; I in them and you in me, that they may be perfected in unity" (17:22–23). We therefore see unified diversity among the Trinity extending to the disciples and the church through the heart of Jesus. Thus, the church receives its power to love from the love that exists among the Trinity.

INTEGRATING THE VERTICAL AND HORIZONTAL DIMENSIONS OF UBUNTU

The problem with the idea of community and *ubuntu* in traditional Africa is that it sometimes leads to a social, institutional unity that misunderstands the basis of true unity. Let us note the following two points:

First, the community of the Trinity does not ignore the personal distinctiveness of its members. In this way, a unified community should embrace its diversity. Beyond seeing others as white, Hispanic, or black, rich or poor, believers should see others as an extension of self. This does not mean that we blur the lines of the other in order to have them fit in our own controlled idea of them. Rather, when the other is an extension of self through biblical *ubuntu*, it means that we have learned to see and *cherish* the differences another person brings to our own experiential being. Second, as the Trinity accomplished the work of salvation at the cross, people from different racial and ethnic groups should embrace at the cross for the sake of unity and the building of their community. If problems occur among believers, or if memories of pain and hatred remain, the victim and the oppressor can meet to seek unity at the cross. This can happen in the following ways:

At the cross the victim meets God and recognizes God's participation in his suffering. Martin Luther King noted that God does not leave us in our agonies and struggles; rather he seeks us in dark places and suffers with us and for us in our tragic prodigality.[36] What encouragement it is for victims to know that God was with them that day when they were oppressed, and that even today the same God is with them binding their wounds from the inside out. When the poor and oppressed identify with Christ, who suffered for and forgave his oppressors, they gain power to forgive. As a result, the cross becomes a place of healing and increased force. The cross is not a sign of weakness, as some may assume; it is the power of God going to the depths of all evil and pain for us. In the same way, the victim who forgives the offender at the cross does not lose force, but regains force.

On the other hand, at this cross the oppressor meets the victim to ask for forgiveness, just as the thief received mercy and forgiveness at the cross (Luke 23:40–43). Here, they do not see each other in terms of ethnicity, social class, or economic ranking, but as children of God who are united after the model of Trinitarian love. At the cross, the victim and the oppressor embrace one another.

Finally, at the cross people from different racial and ethnic groups can present their nations for purification. The innocent blood that has continually been shed through genocides, wars, and rebellions is cursed; for bloodshed pollutes the land (Num 35:33). The solution to this curse is not perpetual violence. The solution is the atonement, which Christ accomplished once for all by shedding his

36. King, *Strength to Love*, cited in Dau, *Suffering and God*, 16.

own blood. Therefore, people should live in unity: not compelled by social norms, but by Christ's love within their hearts. This unity results in increased force for the human race and the strengthening of their nations. Furthermore, Christ is present in their nations and he blesses those nations. Those who do not know Christ's love are drawn to salvation by this blessing, and they join the fellowship of other believers after the manner of *ubuntu*.

CONCLUSION

Understanding the philosophical meaning of *ubuntu* allows us to see why *ubuntu* calls for restorative justice based on forgiveness. The philosophical understanding of *ubuntu* promotes humility as a restorative element in the process of reconciliation. Instead of using punishment as the moral response to injustice, *ubuntu* seeks to restore broken relationships. It seeks a thriving force for the whole community and each person within it.

Ubuntu will be more transformative if we reach from the horizontal dimension to include the vertical, incorporating into our communities the communal love of the Trinity. The cross is the place to experience these transformed relationships: here, the victim and the offender are reconciled. At the cross, they begin to live for one another's restoration and for the restoration of their communities. Here, the blood that has been shed in Rwanda, Burundi, Congo, and elsewhere can be cleansed because God, the Great Umuntu, reconciled the world with himself through Christ, our Great Ancestor.

Africa needs to implement these values, and then share them with a world suffering from ethnic disputes, pluralistic divisions, and economic gaps between the rich and the poor. Every community, every nation, can be blessed by *ubuntu* theology.

At the global level, the philosophy and theology of *ubuntu* is important in today's world for both curative and preventive measures. From a curative perspective, *ubuntu* is needed to bring healing among groups of people who have diminished others in the past so that the victim in the past does not become the oppressor in the future. *Ubuntu* brings healing in the hearts of the victims and the offenders who meet at the cross of Jesus. The blood of Jesus cleanses the fear and shame of the oppressors; it heals the wounds of the victims and gives them grace to live with the life-giving consequences of their forgiveness. The same blood cleanses the curse of innocent blood shed on the land and makes the land a place of worship for people who are reconciled by Jesus and are made ambassadors of reconciliation.

But *ubuntu* is also important because it prevents the dehumanization of the different other today and in the future. Living with the different other is inevitable today. If we do not live with the different other because God has placed us as visitors in a different country, we will live with the different other simply because of globalization. Globalization has brought together people from widely different worldview backgrounds, leading to sociological gaps between tribes and races, the unjust distribution of resources among the rich and poor, the competition of different religious groups, and many other difficult challenges. These challenges impact individuals and communities and bring misunderstandings, conflicts, and divisions.

In view of these challenges, our churches, Christian universities and colleges, and mission organizations in the twenty-first century will have to adopt a theology that acknowledges the value of an individual in community while promoting the relationships these individuals-in-community create—relationships that in turn create a community of harmony and dignity, acknowledging God's image in us all. This is the reason why the theology of *ubuntu* (a person is a person through other persons), if developed upon the communal unity of the Trinity, could be a remedy for these challenges that threaten the beauty of unity in diversity. Only biblical principles of *ubuntu* could make people remain true "human" beings in diverse situations.

But we still haven't dealt with the question of *how* transformation takes place through the different other. I hope you are not tired; let us now turn to chapter 4.

4

Transformation Through the
Different Other

MANY BOOKS SPEAK ABOUT what transformation is, but
few explain how this transformation takes place. My
goal is to show that *ubuntu* is the key to transformation.
Chapters 1 and 2 offered experiences in which I was transformed through the different other. Chapter 3 suggested
a theoretical framework of transformation through the
different other by the use of *ubuntu* philosophy and theology. This chapter offers a practical framework, responding
to the question, "How does transformation through the
different other take place in a practical way?" Let's first of
all define what transformation is before we discuss how it
takes place.

The empirical research I conducted for my doctoral
degree involved twenty-three graduates from two Christian
and two public universities in Kenya. In this study,[1] the
analysis of participants' data defined transformation as "*a
discovery that takes place when one's eyes are opened by a*

---

1. Ntamushobora, *From Transmission to Transformation*, 185.

truth, experience, or inner reflection." These three avenues of thought occur either separately or simultaneously within an encounter with the different other.

Let's take the occurrence of truth. As you may have noticed, it is natural for us human beings to always tend to bring our assumptions into our interpersonal and inter-cultural relationships. When people build arguments on personal beliefs or assumptions, their conclusions could lead to ethnocentrism, a myopia that prevents us from see-ing value in others' cultures. But when we encounter the truth, this new truth opens our inner eyes to a reality that we previously ignored, neglected, or simply did not know about. After such an encounter, we are therefore able to dif-ferentiate between assumption and truth.

Most ethnocentric beliefs are based on assumptions, not on truth. It is an assumption to put people in one box and say, for example, "Black people are lazy" or "White people are imperialistic." When we encounter the different other, we get an opportunity to test our assumptions. Once we know the truth, it changes our old assumptions. We be-come free, for freedom is to know the truth (John 8:32). We then adopt a new perspective that is different from the old one. That is transformation!

So, how about a new experience? Anyone knows by their own experiences that a new experience can also transform us. An African proverb says, "He who has not travelled thinks that his mother is the best cook." I thought that African food was best, but while traveling in the States, I've eaten Mexican and Asian food—and I've loved them; I have been transformed by these experiences.

Finally, regarding inner reflection, there are situa-tions that have made me think twice about my beliefs, and as a result I have been changed through introspection. For instance, teaching undergraduate teenagers at Biola

University has made me reflect more about parenting, and I have come to appreciate my children more than ever before. I have come to notice that teenagers are the same across cultures, and that I was more rigid on my children than I should have been. Teaching teenagers from another culture has transformed my parenting style.

These examples show that transformation takes place when our mind is awakened and begins to think anew. This new realization and freshened perspective becomes a new discovery. I call this discovery *eureka*.

According to Barbara Friberg and Neva Miller, the word *eureka* comes from the Greek verb *euriskō,* which means "a spiritual or intellectual discovery gained through observation, reflection, perception or investigation."[2] This is the reason why exposure to the different other is such an essential part of deep transformation, for it offers an opportunity to *discover*.

An example is when we talk with people who have visited new places. Returning travelers have opportunities now to compare what they knew before the trip with what they discovered while on their journey. I have heard many people who travelled to Africa say that they were amazed to see African Christians rejoicing even though they had so few possessions. This discovery is transformative, for these travelers saw how the deep pulse of God's joy is not tied to how much a person owns.

During my time in the USA, I also found that most of Americans are not emotionally attached to an organization as they are to an individual. They want to connect with "Faustin and Salome" instead of being connected to "TLAfrica." This is a discovery that has transformed me and has affected the way I think about fundraising. I am now aware that Americans want to hear about my life,

2. Friber, Friber, and Miller, *Analytical Lexicon*, 180.

my story, my experiences, and my feelings far more than basic information about our programs in Rwanda, Congo, Burundi, and other countries. They want to hear about the specific story of a widow in Rwanda whose life has been transformed by a cow she received from TLAfrica rather than the general statements about the organization, even if these are also important.

As Christians, when we are reading the Bible and come across a passage that is triggering, we tend to pause and think about it. We reflect on it, or consult a friend or dig it up in a Bible commentary to get the answer. As we discover more about the passage, the scripture comes with transforming power because it was not part of us before. That is why transformation is a succession of discoveries that build upon each other. These new experiences bring clarification to what we already knew, expand our knowledge, and challenge our faith. As Christians, it is those daily discoveries in our lifelong journey with the Lord through his inspired Word and fellowship with him and our fellowship with believers that change us into Christ's likeness. This is why I encourage believers to venture into reading the whole Bible, even books like the Song of Solomon from which people usually shy away.

Another triggering experience could be a testimony that challenges the listener to think and ask questions. My testimony about transformation through suffering has helped believers who are frightened of hardship. After hearing my story, many people have told me, "Faustin, your testimony has challenged my resistance of moving from my comfort zone." A new testimony, especially one that doesn't fit with our cultural or personal concepts of the way God works, can make us uncomfortable. We start to ask ourselves if we have projected personal values onto God, and in this way others' stories shake off the chaff in our souls, and help us press into a grace that surprises us in its many forms and faces. Encountering the different other helps us hear different stories and testimonies, which can in turn make us reflect on what that means for our personal lives and situations. And this kind of reflection changes our lives.

But *eureka* could also be triggered by a shocking observation or a provoking thought. One shocking observation I have made from my life in the USA is that while Africans are a community that is characterized by shame, Americans are not. When I would walk through Biola's campus, I would see young people kissing each other, and people took it as normal. If you visit Uganda Christian University or Daystar University in Kenya, you would never see young people kissing each other in public. It is shameful. This shocking observation has transformed my cultural anthropology. I now take it as acceptable, even if I do not endorse it. I can now say, "It is okay for young Americans to do so," but I wouldn't have been able to say this five years ago. Interaction with Americans has changed my perspective. My new perspective is that it all depends on the heart's motivation. Young people not kissing each other in public may be doing terrible things in private.

Also, transformation can be triggered by a provoking thought. This is one way Africans mentor young people. If a father wants to provoke his son to begin thinking about marriage, he would, for example, call the son and tell him, "You know so and so, son of so and so; do you know that you were born the same season, when we were harvesting corn? Do you know that if your friend dies today his name would remain? But if you die today your name would not. Go and think about it."

Jesus used provoking thoughts in his teaching. For instance, in Mark 2:1–13 Jesus told the paralytic man, "Son, your sins are forgiven." That was provocative for the

Pharisees who were present. Eventually, they thought in their hearts that what Jesus said was blasphemy. Jesus, knowing what they were thinking, confronted them on the spot and demonstrated his authority by healing the paralytic. In verse 12, the healing of the paralytic "amazed everyone and they praised God saying, 'We have never seen anything like this!'"

In all of the above situations, the truth, knowledge, or experience brings newness in one's thinking, feeling, beliefs, and relationships with self, others, and God. Let me illustrate this with my own experience.

On December 19, 1979, after I heard a sermon from 2 Corinthians 5:17, I discovered that I was a sinner and decided to put my faith in Christ. I became a new creation. This newness heralded new thinking, feeling, belief and relationship with myself, others, and God. From that day onward I understood the difference between being in Christ and being in a religion. Previously, I was in a religion that made me enjoy meeting others on a Sunday, and singing in the choir with other young boys and girls. But after the new experience, I understood that to be in Christ means to surrender oneself to him for total control. Also, from that day onward I felt peace in my life. I accepted myself as I was. As I continued to read the Bible, I felt more freedom to live the Christian life. Before then, reading the Bible was a burden. I now felt more joy to live a life without the pleasures of the flesh that come with the addiction of sin. Furthermore, my beliefs changed. Before my salvation, I was shy to confess a weakness. But after salvation I found that confessing is not a weakness, but a strength that comes from the work of the Holy Spirit in my heart.

Ultimately, my salvation had implications for my relationship with myself, others, and God. I accepted myself as I was more than I could do before, but also I began to see others as created in God's image, as sinners who can be forgiven as I myself was forgiven. Finally, I began to put God first in my life and follow his guidance rather than following my impulses.

TRANSMISSION AND TRANSFORMATION

Many people have asked me, "Why is it that people in the world know that tribalism and racism are bad, but practice them—even in Christian organizations?" My professor who was reading about *ubuntu* and the call for Africans to choose inclusion rather than exclusion of the other also wanted to know what I thought about the fact that despite *ubuntu*, Africa continues to be the region with the most strife. The answer is that it is not enough to know the truth; the truth needs to sink down from the head to the heart before it is applied.

Take the example of Peter's sermon on the day of Pentecost in Acts 2. Peter's sermon was not just about transmission of information, but about transformation of lives. He preached truth that changed the thoughts of his listeners. They now understood that the coming of the Holy Spirit was the fulfillment of God's promise and Joel's prophecy (Acts 2:15–21), that the risen Christ is the Messiah and Son of David (2:22–31), and that the risen Christ is the fulfillment of the prophecy (2:32–36). But Peter's transformative sermon did not stop there.

It is not enough to know that Hutu and Tutsi are created in the same image of God and that they come from the same ancestor. To be transformative, this truth should move from the head to the heart. For Peter, changed thoughts awakened emotions (2:37–41). Knowing without conviction is like a seed in dry land. Emotions are like water, which makes the seed germinate in the soil. When in Acts 2:37 the Jews asked Peter, "Brother, what shall we do?"

we can see how transformation was moving from head to heart, getting ready to stimulate theoretical knowledge into *action*. Emotions are therefore bridges between knowledge (truth) and action (experience).

Transformation = Truth + Emotion + Will = Action

When Peter said, "Repent and be baptized" (2:38), he was helping the hearers to put into action their changed thoughts and awakened emotion. Repentance takes place when one understands the truth, for the truth changes thoughts, changed thoughts awaken emotions, and awakened emotions move a person to action. Of course, one needs to be willing to take that action, and action draws from new and empowering perspective. For example, as one moves towards repentance, one first understands that he or she is a sinner (truth). This recognition is followed by an inner repugnance towards sin (emotion), and the emotion ignites the will to forsake the sinful nature and to surrender to God (action).

Applied to transformation through the different other, there is need for one to know the background and worldview of the other person, and this comes from spending time with the different other in genuine dialogue. It also involves examining one's assumptions toward the other person's worldview. At this level, we are searching for truth. Once we know the truth, we can remain at that level, and have a head full of knowledge without any positive action. But there is also the possibility that this new truth will lead to some emotion, such as worry, concern, sadness, frustration, confusion, or other emotions like affection, delight, empathy, and care. These emotions thus prompt the person to change—indeed, they are the water on the soil of the heart, nurturing that seed of encounter with the different other. With water, seed, and soil now together, the presence of new life—the miracle of change—occurs. The person can now accept the different other as he or she is, or love him or her unconditionally, or will to learn from the different other's worldview so that the two persons can enrich each other from a rendezvous of giving and receiving, which leads to new perspectives.

It is important to acknowledge that transformation begins with a disorientating dilemma. Theorists of transformative learning like Jack Mezirow,[3] Patricia Cranton,[4] and Stephen Brookfield[5] help explain that often before positive emotions there are confusing or negative emotions. This is especially true when it comes to transformation through the different other. It is always uneasy to relate to a person from a different tribe, race, or worldview. We assume our presuppositions are truth. But once we know the new person and see the truth about his or her reality, fear is transformed. We pass from simply accepting the other person to deepening our relationship with him or her through concrete actions.

THE POWER OF TRANSFORMATION THROUGH THE OTHER

The findings from my research indicate that the light that opens one's eyes comes from the Holy Spirit and passes through the other (a person or written material from another person) for one to receive it. Some participants in the research stated that they were transformed through reading books or dissertations. Written material constitutes

3. Mezirow, *Learning as Transformation.*

4. Cranton, *Understanding and promoting transformative learning: A guide for educators of adults.*

5. Brookfield, *Skillful Teacher.*

reflection in critical thinking. Self-reflection can also come through reading a book, such as the Bible. The Holy Spirit, whom I call the Great Other, works through the written Word of God to transform the reader. However, the majority of participants stated that they had been transformed through the other. As I mentioned earlier, this reflects the communal worldview of Africans, which values relationships above written materials. The other could be the self (self as object or "me," as opposed to self as subject or "I"), another person (familiar or unfamiliar), or the Holy Spirit himself.

The familiar other was mainly colleagues, students, and professors. On the one hand, as professors taught in a transformative way, they challenged the learners to think and change their perspectives. As professors mentored learners through small groups and fellowships, learners were enabled to see further than they would before. As professors exhibited humility before their protégés, the learners became more humble. On the other hand, as learners saw their colleagues' commitment, they were challenged. As they heard different views from their colleagues, they came to appreciate diversity in culture and in ways of thinking. The same was said for participants who were challenged by listening to people from totally different views. Opposing ideas would make the participants think twice, even if they would not agree.

In addition to being transformed through the familiar other, participants stated that they were transformed through the unfamiliar other. For instance, participants stated that interacting with colleagues from different denominations was eye opening. This transformation came as a result of learning to stop judging those from different denominations and appreciating them. Also, guest speakers were said to have challenged some participants. The visit of some renowned guest speakers would give an opportunity to learners to interact with them when it would have been difficult to reach them in other ways.

In addition to being transformed through the other—familiar or unfamiliar—the participants stated that they were transformed through self-discovery. Self-discovery could come through the process of making personal decisions, through introspection, and through becoming aware of how ignorant one is. These situations made participants examine themselves, which led to transformation. But furthermore, self-discovery also took place as participants made shocking observations, as they accepted themselves as they were, as they appreciated their cultures, and as they identified themselves with their people.

For participants, the aim of transformation was not self-ambition, but rather serving the other in the community and helping the other change perspective. The former was done through initiating development projects for the community and serving on school boards—as well as denying one's ambitions for a good job outside of the community in order to live and serve among one's people. The latter was done through equipping the community members with the Word of God, mentoring other people, loving and accepting those who do not share one's opinion as one agrees to disagree in love. Empowering and mentoring others could be done either through relationship or written material.

TRANSFORMATION THROUGH SHARPENING ONE ANOTHER

One of the best verses in the Bible that explains the principle of the other as my extension and not as my exclusion is Proverbs 27:17: "As iron sharpens iron, so a man sharpens the countenance of his friend." The Talmud applied this verse to study, as two students sharpening each other in the study of the Torah.[6] It has, therefore, a direct application to two or more students, disciples, of the Word of God.

Let us use the analogy of an African sword that sharpens another to understand the usefulness of sharpening one another for spiritual transformation as Proverbs 27:17 says. An African sword is kept in a scabbard so that it may remain sharp and does not harm anyone. It is drawn from its scabbard only when it is needed for use. Suppose that we have two swords that are kept in the scabbards—can these two swords sharpen each other? Of course not! Even if one sword is removed from its scabbard but the other is not, the swords cannot sharpen each other. When the two swords are removed from their scabbards, then they can sharpen each other without a problem. When sharpening each other, both swords become sharp and lose their bluntness. Some bluntness may even require that swords be sharpened several times.

From this analogy we learn the following lesson: unless the heart is removed from its scabbard, it cannot be sharpened. This means that unless there is trust between fellow believers, we will not be sharing enough of ourselves for transformation to happen. Also, if only one person discloses and the other person does not, this could hinder true relationship development between the two and could hinder deep and continual transformation.

The community of believers in Acts 2 was like a laboratory for experimenting and practicing what the apostles were teaching. This happened as disciples studied the Word of God together, lived together, interacted with one another, questioned each other, blessed each other—and probably often offended each other and had to work through conflicts. Sharpening can be uncomfortable and difficult, as we have seen, but building relationships in which we are

6. Ross, *Proverbs*, 219.

not always hiding within our scabbards gives us the chance to create a community where each person's *real* self matters for the sake of all of us together. This is practical, enduring Trinitarian love.

Indeed, most of the time reconciliation—either tribal or racial—does not bear positive results because those involved have a political agenda rather than the hope for transformation. Countries in Africa that have gone through civil wars would rarely admit that people have wounds in their hearts that need healing. Even in the States, churches and universities shy away from openly discussing issues related to tribalism and racism. Some universities with one race majority may try to put some images of the minority race on their website to show there is some representation of the minority race. Some universities even organize racial education talks and workshops but fail to touch the real issues of the heart.

To return to our analogy, these talks may ask participants to put their swords on the table, but removing the swords from the scabbards is another matter. It is so painful to expose our blunt, bloody swords to each other, and all the more painful when we begin to truly dialogue and sharpen these swords together. This is why believers need to be purposeful in creating a place where trust cultivates this kind of exposure and interaction. Thank the Lord that his Holy Spirit is here to help us!

THE PLACE OF THE HOLY SPIRIT IN TRANSFORMATION

As seen in chapter 3, man does not have the capacity to love the different other. If he does, it is often for some social reasons, which are not transformative. Loving the different other can only be transformative if it comes from a changed heart. Yet, only God can change man's heart and give him true love for the different other.

Also, the process of changing from one's old assumptions to new assumptions— repentance in biblical terms— is not man's task, but the Holy Spirit's task. Repentance is a personal decision that one makes in response to the Holy Spirit's conviction of our sins. The moment we make that voluntary decision, something new takes place: salvation begins new birth, continues with sanctification and culminates with glorification. Let's illustrate this with the example of Peter's sermon on the day of Pentecost. The truth that Peter preached was communicated in the power of the Holy Spirit in a way that the same Holy Spirit caused disequilibrium in the assumptions of the hearers. They therefore began to critically assess their old assumptions.

While a good teacher and good methods help lead to transformation, the ultimate source and agent of transformation is the Holy Spirit of God, who works as catalyst during the communication process between the communicator and the receiver. The Holy Spirit is the one who causes transformation to take place in the mind and heart of an individual. Good teachers can help develop others' thinking, but they cannot change others' hearts. It is the Holy Spirit who transforms people's hearts through a supernatural new birth leading to everlasting life.

Without this new birth in a person's heart, transformation is incomplete and not lasting. After the new birth, the Holy Spirit continues to work in a person's life until he or she reaches full maturity in Christ (Eph 4: 13). This is the reason why we stated that without a vertical dimension of *ubuntu*, it can remain a humanistic and social practice without lasting results. Transformation through the different other can therefore only truly happen through the Holy Spirit working through someone who accepts his leading.

The Holy Spirit is the author of transformation. He is a teacher who brings understanding and illumination, knowledge, and wisdom. But he is also a comforter who encourages the learner in his or her weaknesses and difficulties. He is a guide who gives direction to the Christian learner when confronted with various choices to make. Finally, he is the one who encourages us to learn from those around us with humility and wisdom, so we can grow in ways we could not on our own.

CONCLUSION

How does transformation through the different other take place? God uses the different other to challenge me, to teach me new truths, to help me see my ignorance and myopia, and to ask myself questions that lead to change. The more one is exposed to the different other, the more he or she has opportunities to be sharpened—but this begins with intentional willingness to be sharpened by the other. This willingness requires humility and vulnerability to admit one's limitations and ignorance, and once this happens, the different other brings opportunities for a paradigm shift in the way one thinks, feels, and acts. Intercultural exposures are invisible books with invisible truths touching invisible places of the mind and heart, making the person exposed grow through experiences that bring lasting transformation.

We are now moving to the conclusion of the book, in which I will offer ten principles of transformation through the different other.

5

Conclusion: Ten Principles

THIS CHAPTER RECAPITULATES THE four previous chapters and gives ten key lessons from the entire book. In chapters 1 and 2 we stated that the root cause of racial and tribal problems is not really the difference in color, but the human heart. We however admitted that differences in race, tribe, and worldview could widen the gap in people's hearts and cause more separation and strife. We saw how the human being can use his heart to hurt his fellow human beings. But we also saw that the same heart, if transformed by the Great Other, can shape and sharpen the heart of his follow human beings.

As a result of the human fall (Genesis 3), we are all strangers to one another and to God. Whether or not we share or do not share the same color and worldview, we are all strangers to ourselves, to one another and to God. We do not understand ourselves and so we cannot understand others who are different from us. We judge others because we do not see their reality, unless it is revealed to us by the Great Other, who is the Truth and the Reality. All of us fall short of God's glory (Rom 3:23), and thus we all need some of this glorious light from the Great Other to illuminate our hearts so that we may understand ourselves and others, and may accept ourselves and others as we are.

In being a stranger to ourselves and to others, especially those who are different from us, we tend to seek comfortable space by communing with those whose values are similar to ours, and by so doing we unfortunately miss the blessing of being sharpened by someone different from us. When we emerge from this fear, however, we are able to approach the different other for the rendezvous of giving and receiving, and as a result we became co-workers, co-teachers and co-heirs of God's kingdom. It is at this level that we can say, "It is not about me, my color or my worldview, but God's kingdom and his Body, of which there are many parts that are different from me but complimentary to me."

It is worth remembering that no man is an island. Community is very important for our transformation. Yet community implies diversity. Any community has a diversity of personalities, ages, sexes, and perspectives, and often races or ethnicities and modes of communication. Diversity in community, when developed with a sense of unity, can shape us into vessels that glorify the Lord by pouring into and receiving from those who are different from us.

The best place to share this community life is within the family. I can testify to this truth as a Christian husband and father. My wife and children have molded me into what I am today more than any information I have received from great mentors in my life. My heart has learned to be patient with my wife when she delays. I have learned to listen to her when she has expressed different opinions, and I have learned to listen to my children when they have complained against my many rules. Living among my family members has been a profound school for my heart.

That is the same for any community, especially for a Christian community of believers whose lives can sharpen each other using God's truth and wisdom. Robert Saucy acknowledges that "the normal spiritual growth or transformation of the believer takes place as the life-giving grace of Christ flows through the members of his body through their fellowship."[1] Explaining how this transformation takes place, Saucy points out, "In community we learn to live God's transforming truth together, gaining insight into its meaning from one another and being mentored in living it out in differing situations." He adds, "We get to know Christ through others and learn to live out the Christian story with them."[2]

As I shared earlier, I was transformed just by seeing how young Americans in my class loved each other, despite their differences in color. It gives me hope that as our young people continue to be impacted by the love of Christ, and with proper teaching from their families color will not be something to guide people in their decisions. The same hope applies to Africans. Young people in Rwanda, Congo, Uganda, Kenya, and other countries who are not corrupted by the poisonous teaching of their family members have more chances to be peacemakers. That is why in Africa we need young scholars, managers, and leaders to become part of their communities, teaching the value of diversity and showing it as a way for transformation. This is my passion!

Another important point is that often we miss transformation through the different other because of pride. When we think that we do not need the different other because he or she does not share our cultural values, or just because we do not want to learn from the person because it seems like too much work and discomfort, then we are

1. Saucy, *Mending the Heart*, 243.
2. Ibid.

acting out of pride. Yet, as the Greeks said, humility is the crown of all the virtues. It is humility that made Christ, the king of kings, succeed in his salvation mission when he chose to learn from the human beings he had created (his earthly mother Mary and his caring father Joseph), and to become like them in order to transform them. That was selfless humility. While transformation through the different other can be viewed as unimportant from a utilitarian perspective (what shall I get from him or her?), for Christians it is not only what we get, but also what we give to another. This is love!

Finally, God will allow us to go through negative experiences so that we may draw nearer to him in times of need. I do not remember praying so much in the USA as during the seventeen weeks and two days that my family was away! Nor does my family remember any time in the USA that we fasted and prayed more than during the time of need when Jesus visited my family and sent his messenger to give us $1,000. No one has again given us such an amount of money! My family has learned to be content with little in a culture that has plenty—and that is not easy. But I am sure our testimony has been a blessing to the different others who cry that they are poor when they do not lack food in their refrigerators and have medical insurance. Our children have come closer to God in the USA than when we were in Africa, because tuition for their education is always a miracle.

Chapter 3 established a theoretical foundation on which to build this transformation through the different other. We used the *ubuntu* philosophy because it values individuals and communities. The philosophy and theology of *ubuntu* is important in today's world for both curative and preventive measures. From a curative perspective, *ubuntu* is needed to bring healing among groups of people who have hurt others in the past so that the victim in the past does not become the oppressor in the future. We noticed that *ubuntu* is important because it prevents the dehumanization of the different other today and in the future.

However, *ubuntu* gives lasting results only when it can move from merely the social (horizontal) dimension to embracing the spiritual (vertical) dimension, which is change of the heart. This is the only way *ubuntu* can bring healing to the hearts of the victims and offenders who meet at the cross of Jesus.

In chapter 4 we highlighted practical ways transformation through the other can become reality. Using empirical finding from my research, we found that transformation takes place through the other, written material, and self-reflection, but that the other had the most transformational impact. Also, we saw that the Holy Spirit is the transformer *par excellence*. This supports the idea that in order for *ubuntu* to be transformative, there should be a vertical dimension of relationship between individuals and God.

TEN PRINCIPLES

Now, I would like to offer ten principles of transformation through the different other so that we can achieve a true rendezvous of giving and receiving:

Principle One: As you plan to meet people from a different race, tribe, or worldview, remember that people all over the world are fallen like you, struggling with the same problems of self-gratification. The human heart is deceitful above all things and beyond all cure!

Principle Two: A human being has the capacity to consume or commune with another human being. While it is true that the heart can be deceitful beyond measure, the opposite can also be true: the heart of the different other can be a blessing to one's growth, becoming a continuation of me—an inclusion that makes "I" and "You" a community of two different interdependent hearts capable of sharpening each other. This is possible because only life can shape life.

Principle Three: An uneasy relationship with the different other could lead to maturity in Christ. God may allow you to go through uneasy times when relating with the different other or a different environment for his glory and for your good.

Principle Four: Human beings are powerless to bring transformation into their own lives. Transformation only comes when we allow the Holy Spirit's light to reveal things about our heart that we need to know. Then we can understand how we have fallen short of God's glory, repent and confess our sin, and allow new perspectives to germinate—perspectives that deepen our love for God and for others.

Principle Five: Knowing that the different other brings transformation is not enough. Change happens when we know the truth, and that knowledge sinks down into our heart until it moves us to new actions. It is therefore important that we purposefully set out to know new truths and new people in an authentic and emotional way, so that we resist only gathering mind knowledge of others.

Principle Six: The different other can be transformative only if we allow him or her to sharpen us. This means that we need to open our heart to the different other. This requires trust—or taking a risk. When we open up to the different other and vice versa, a rendezvous of giving and receiving takes place in both lives, and both lives become transformed. The trust, acceptance, and care for each other that results from this rendezvous creates a space not just for personal growth, but also for emotional healing, especially when one notices that "not everyone different from me is against me." This is the kind of healing that expands into communities and brings healing throughout a nation.

Principle Seven: Relating with the different other is difficult. The relationship does not even guarantee that it will lead to transformation. Rather than leading to healing, it may lead to hurting. In this case, the cross becomes a healing place where those with broken hearts can meet and receive inner surgery through forgiveness. Even in these circumstances, though, a person's heart has the chance to connect more deeply to God's love as well as become mature, and thus more durable for future bumps on the road to loving community.

Principle Eight: The Lord is seeking people who can serve as bridges for a rendezvous of giving and receiving that he is intentionally creating through globalization. People can become bridges when they are ready to change from "I am" to "we are" and from "my" to "our." They are those who are open to accept the other as their extension. These are the people who will become global peacemakers. However, these global peacemakers should not compromise the truth of the Word of God for the sake of adjusting to the world. As peacemakers following the example of Christ, grace and truth should always kiss each other in our relationship with the different other.

Principle Nine: Churches and Christian institutions that are hesitant to accept the different other may be surprised when circumstances insist that they accommodate the different others because of globalization. It may not be the most constructive context for these institutions to grow if they are compelled by external factors to live with different others. But if this is the case, openness to the Holy Spirit will help the leaders of these institutions navigate unfamiliar and seemingly scary waters. God certainly uses external factors—but as the Israelites in the desert learned, change of heart this way can mean a longer and more difficult journey. Let us seek where the Holy Spirit is working now!

Principle Ten: Relating with the different other is the best way for believers to prepare themselves for the time when every tongue and every tribe and every race will stand together, singing praises to the Lamb of God who was slain for the redemption of every person from every nation. Relating with the different other is God's will and intent. Let us prepare for such a time, then, and seek God's glory through loving the different other!

Afterword

I HAVE ALWAYS STRUGGLED to see Africans become self-reliant. In my article published in the *EMQ* in October 2003, I mentioned that we Africans needed to be self-reliant for "our self-esteem, dignity, identity and self-respect." Otherwise, as I wrote, "If we Africans do not think about our situation and seek a way to self-support, we will continue to be called beggars, and so will our children."[1] That is the tragedy that needs to be stopped!

"Africa is the richest continent," Adeyemo pointed out, "but Africans are among the poorest on the globe."[2] The good news is that Africans are working hard to break this paradox. Africa needs education that is holistic. We need education that trains graduates to think critically and love the Lord and others—an education that empowers them to bring transformation in their communities. This education must be relevant to the needs of people and should use a curriculum and materials that speak to the souls of the learners. This is my vision for the rest of my life. Now that I have finished my doctoral studies, I would like to continue serving my people through TLAfrica. The board and I also have a vision to begin a university in Rwanda whose mission will be to train graduates with the same philosophy of

1. Ntamushobora, *Toward Self-reliance: A challenge for churches and ministries in Africa*, 490

2. Adeyemo, *Africa's enigma.*

holistic transformation. But we would like to build this vision on a sustainable foundation so that in the future, even without funds from the West, the ministry may continue.

All the funds from the sale of this book will go toward the sustainability project for TLAfrica. Our short-term vision is to begin working on a complete core curriculum for all our non-formal leadership training programs and for the proposed university as we at the same time develop self-reliant projects for the organization. Using participatory development practice, my fellow board members and I will all be involved in seeking God's will on the right projects that could generate funds, the right place to develop them, and the right ways to manage them. By doing so, all the stakeholders will grow together in intercultural leadership and management skills, and our unity will lead to the true *ubuntu* that is needed to transform our African people into disciples of Christ who glorify the Lord in their lives and bless other people from the rest of the globe with all kinds of blessings, including financial blessings.

As you buy a copy of this book, you are partnering with me to achieve this vision. You can mobilize your Bible study group, your class (for students), your university, or your entire school or local church to purchase copies of the book. But you can also give toward self-reliance for the organization so that we may achieve this vision. Please visit our website at www.tlafrica.org.

Amahoro – Shalom!
Faustin Ntamushobora, PhD
President, TLAfrica, Inc.

Bibliography

Abadeer, Adel, S. "Seeking Redemptive Diversity in Christian Institutions of Higher Education: Challenges and Hopes from Within." *Christian Higher Education* 8/3 (August 2009) 187–202.

Adeyemo, Tokunboh. "Africa's Enigma." In *Faith in Development: Partnership between the World Bank and the Churches of Africa*, edited by Deryke Belshaw, Robert Calderisi, and Chris Sugden, 31–38. Delhi: World Bank, Regnum Books, 2001.

———. *Is Africa Cursed?* Nairobi: Christian Learning Material Centre, 1997.

Ashcroft, Bill, Gareth Griffiths, and Helen Tiffin. *Post-Colonial Studies: The Key Concepts*. 2nd ed. New York: Routledge, 2000.

Bassey, Magnus O. *Western Education and Political Domination in Africa: A Study in Critical and Dialogical Pedagogy*. Westport, CT: Bergin & Garvey, 1999.

Bennetts, Christine. "The Impact of Transformational Learning on Individuals, Families and Communities." *International Journal of Lifelong Education* 22/5 (September 2003) 457–80.

Bailey, Sarah Pulliam. "African Scholar Tokunboh Adeyemo Dies." Gleanings, a blog of *Christianity Today*, March 18, 2010. Online: http://blog.christianitytoday.com/ctliveblog/archives/2010/03/african_scholar.html.

Battle, Michael. *Reconciliation: The Ubuntu theology of Desmond Tutu*. Cleveland: Pilgrim, 1997.

Berg, Vanden. "Bonhoeffer's Discipleship: Theology for the Purpose of Christian Formation." *Calvin Theological Journal* 44/2 (2009) 333–49.

Brookfield, Stephen D. *The Skillful Teacher: On Technique, Trust, and Responsiveness in the Classroom*. San Francisco: Jossey-Bass, 1990.

Buber, Martin. *I and Thou*. Translated by Ronald Gregor Smith. 2nd ed. Edinburgh: T. & T. Clark, 1958.

Bibliography

Burtness, James. *Shaping the Future: The Ethics of Dietrich Bonhoeffer*. Philadelphia: Fortress, 1985.

Césaire, Aimé. *Discourse on Colonialism*. New York: Monthly Review Press, 2000.

Charry, Ellen T. *By the Renewing of Your Minds: The Pastoral Function of Christian Doctrine*. New York: Oxford University Press, 1997.

Clark, Janine. "Learning from the Past: Three Lessons from the Rwandan Genocide." *African Studies* 68/1 (March 2009) 1–28.

Conn, Harvie M., and Manuel Ortiz. *Urban Ministry: The Kingdom, the City, & the People of God*. Illinois: InterVarsity, 2001.

Cranton, Patricia. *Understanding and Promoting Transformative Learning: A Guide for Educators of Adults*. 2nd ed. San Francisco: Jossey-Bass, 2006.

Dau, Isaiah Majok. *Suffering and God: A Theological Reflection on the War in Sudan*. Nairobi: Pauline, 2002.

Draper, Robert. "Rift in Paradise." *National Geographic* 220/5 (2011) 82–117.

Edgar, Brian. *The Message of the Trinity: Life in God*. Downers Grove, IL: InterVarsity, 2004.

Ester, Peter, Michael Braun, and Peter Mohler. *Globalization, Value Change, and Generations: A Cross-National and Intergenerational Perspective*. Leiden: Brill, 2006.

Foster, Richard J., and Kathryn A. Helmers. *Life with God: Reading the Bible for Spiritual Transformation*. New York: Harper, 2008.

Friber, Timothy, Barbara Friberg, and Neva Miller. *Analytical Lexicon of the Greek New Testament*. Grand Rapids: Baker, 2000.

Graham, Billy. *The Key to Personal Peace*. Nashville: T. Nelson, 2003.

Hatzfield, Jean. *A Time for Machetes: The Rwandan Genocide: The Killers Speak: A Report*. London: Farrar, Straus, and Giroux, 2005.

Hohenberg, Paul M., and Lynn Hollen Lees. *The Making of Urban Europe: 1000–1994*. Cambridge, MA: Harvard University Press, 1995.

Horrell, J. Scott. "The Eternal Son of God in the Social Trinity." In *Jesus in Trinitarian Perspective: An Intermediate Christology*, by Fred Sanders and Klaus Dieter Issler, 44–79. Nashville: B & H, 2007.

Hurtado, Albert L., and Peter Iverson, editors. *Major Problems in American Indian History: Documents and Essays*. Lexington, MA: D.C. Heath and Company, 1994.

Icenogle, Gareth Weldon. *Biblical Foundations for Small Group Ministry: An Integrative Approach*. Westmont, IL: InterVarsity, 1994.

Jayakumar, Uma M. "Can Higher Education Meet the Needs of an Increasingly Diverse and Global Society?: Campus Diversity and Cross-Cultural Competencies." *Harvard Educational Review* 78/4 (2008) 615–51.

Jenkins, Philip. *The Next Christendom: The Coming of global Christianity*. New York: Oxford University Press, 2002.

Kasyoka, John M. M. *An Introduction to Philosophy of Religion*. Eldoret, Kenya: Zapf Chancery, 2008.

King, Roberta R. "Under the Mango Tree: Worship, Song and Spiritual Transformation in Africa." In *Worship That Changes Lives: Multidisciplinary and congregational Perspectives on Spiritual Transformation*, edited by Alexis D.Abernethy, 141–66. Grand Rapids: Baker Academic, 2008.

Krapiec, Mieczyslaw Albert. *Person and Natural Law*. Translated by Maria Szymanska. New York: Peter Lang, 1993.

Lewis, C. S. *Mere Christianity*. New York: Macmillan, 1960.

Lingenfelter, Judith, and Sherwood G. Lingenfelter. *Teaching Cross-Culturally: An Incarnational Model for Learning and Teaching*. Grand Rapids: Baker Academic, 2003.

Lingenfelter, Sherwood, G. *Leading Cross-Culturally: Covenant Relationships for Effective Christian Leadership*. Grand Rapids: Baker Academic, 2008.

Longman, Timothy Paul. *Christianity and Genocide in Rwanda*. New York : Cambridge University Press, 2010.

Mbiti, John S. *Concepts of God in Africa*. New York: Praeger, 1970.

Mezirow, Jack. *Learning as Transformation: Critical Perspectives on a Theory in Progress*. San Francisco: Jossey-Bass, 2000.

Milligan, W. J. *The New Nomads: Challenges Facing Christians in Western Europe*. Geneva, Switzerland: World Council of Churches, 1984.

Mironko, Charles. "Ibitero: Means and Motive in the Rwandan Genocide." In *Genocide in Cambodia and Rwanda: New Perspectives*, edited by Susan E. Cook, 163–89. New Brunswick, NJ: Transaction, 2006.

Ntamushobora, Faustin. *From Transmission to Transformation: An Exploration of Education for Holistic Transformation in Selected Christian and Public University in Kenya*. PhD diss., Biola University, May 2012.

———. "Towards Self-Reliance: A Challenge for African Churches and Ministries." *Evangelical Missions Quarterly* 39/4 (2003) 490–95.

Otabil, Mensa. *Beyond the Rivers of Ethiopia*. Accra: Altar International, 1992.

Bibliography

Ortiz, Manuel, and Susan Baker, editors. *The Urban Face of Mission: Ministering the Gospel in a Diverse and Changing World*. Philipsburg, NJ: P & R, 2002.

Prior, David. *The Message of 1 Corinthians: Life in the Local Church*. Downers Grove, IL: InterVarsity, 1985.

Rahim, M. Afzalur, Gabriel F. Buntzman, and Douglas White. "An Empirical Study of the Stages of Moral Development and Conflict Management Styles." *International Journal of Conflict Management* 10/2 (1999) 154–71.

Ross, P. Allen. "Proverbs." *The Expositor's Bible Commentary: Proverbs–Isaiah*, edited by Tremper Longman III and Garland E. David, 21–252. Rev. ed. Grand Rapids: Zondervan, 2008.

Saucy, L. R. *Mending the Heart: The Way of Spiritual Transformation*. Forthcoming, 2013.

Stinton, Diana B. *Jesus of Africa: Voices of Contemporary African Christology*. Nairobi: Pauline, 2004.

Stone, Dan, editor. *The Historiography of Genocide*. New York: Palgrave Macmillan, 2008.

Verderber, F. R. *Communicate!* Belmont, CA: Wadsworth, 1985.

Verwoerd, Wilhelm. "Individual and/or Social Justice after Apartheid?: The South African Truth and Reconciliation Commission." *European Journal of Development Research* 11/2 (1999) 115–42.

Volf, Miroslav. *Exclusion and Embrace: A Theological Exploration of Identity, Otherness, and Reconciliation*. Nashville: Abingdon, 1996.

Wengert, Timothy J., editor. *The Pastoral Luther: Essays on Martin Luther's Practical Theology*. Grand Rapids: Eerdmans, 2009.